AT THE NEXUS OF CYBERSECURITY AND PUBLIC POLICY

Some Basic Concepts and Issues

David Clark, Thomas Berson, and Herbert S. Lin, *Editors*

Committee on Developing a Cybersecurity Primer:
Leveraging Two Decades of National Academies Work

Computer Science and Telecommunications Board

NATIONAL RESEARCH COUNCIL
OF THE NATIONAL ACADEMIES

THE NATIONAL ACADEMIES PRESS
Washington, D.C.
www.nap.edu

THE NATIONAL ACADEMIES PRESS   500 Fifth Street, NW   Washington, DC 20001

NOTICE: The project that is the subject of this report was approved by the Governing Board of the National Research Council, whose members are drawn from the councils of the National Academy of Sciences, the National Academy of Engineering, and the Institute of Medicine. The members of the committee responsible for the report were chosen for their special competences and with regard for appropriate balance.

Support for this project was provided by the National Science Foundation under Award Number CNS-0940372. Additional support was provided by Microsoft Corporation, Google, Inc., and the President's Committee of the National Academies.

Any opinions, findings, or conclusions expressed in this publication are those of the author(s) and do not necessarily reflect the views of the organizations or agencies that provided support for the project.

International Standard Book Number 13:   978-0-309-30318-7
International Standard Book Number 10:   0-309-30318-4
Library of Congress Control Number: 2014940211

This report is available from

Computer Science and Telecommunications Board
National Research Council
500 Fifth Street, NW
Washington, DC 20001

Additional copies of this report are available from the National Academies Press, 500 Fifth Street, NW, Keck 360, Washington, DC 20001; (800) 624-6242 or (202) 334-3313; http://www.nap.edu.

Printed in the United States of America

THE NATIONAL ACADEMIES
Advisers to the Nation on Science, Engineering, and Medicine

The **National Academy of Sciences** is a private, nonprofit, self-perpetuating society of distinguished scholars engaged in scientific and engineering research, dedicated to the furtherance of science and technology and to their use for the general welfare. Upon the authority of the charter granted to it by the Congress in 1863, the Academy has a mandate that requires it to advise the federal government on scientific and technical matters. Dr. Ralph J. Cicerone is president of the National Academy of Sciences.

The **National Academy of Engineering** was established in 1964, under the charter of the National Academy of Sciences, as a parallel organization of outstanding engineers. It is autonomous in its administration and in the selection of its members, sharing with the National Academy of Sciences the responsibility for advising the federal government. The National Academy of Engineering also sponsors engineering programs aimed at meeting national needs, encourages education and research, and recognizes the superior achievements of engineers. Dr. C. D. Mote, Jr., is president of the National Academy of Engineering.

The **Institute of Medicine** was established in 1970 by the National Academy of Sciences to secure the services of eminent members of appropriate professions in the examination of policy matters pertaining to the health of the public. The Institute acts under the responsibility given to the National Academy of Sciences by its congressional charter to be an adviser to the federal government and, upon its own initiative, to identify issues of medical care, research, and education. Dr. Harvey V. Fineberg is president of the Institute of Medicine.

The **National Research Council** was organized by the National Academy of Sciences in 1916 to associate the broad community of science and technology with the Academy's purposes of furthering knowledge and advising the federal government. Functioning in accordance with general policies determined by the Academy, the Council has become the principal operating agency of both the National Academy of Sciences and the National Academy of Engineering in providing services to the government, the public, and the scientific and engineering communities. The Council is administered jointly by both Academies and the Institute of Medicine. Dr. Ralph J. Cicerone and Dr. C. D. Mote, Jr., are chair and vice chair, respectively, of the National Research Council.

www.national-academies.org

COMMITTEE ON DEVELOPING A CYBERSECURITY PRIMER: LEVERAGING TWO DECADES OF NATIONAL ACADEMIES WORK

DAVID CLARK, Massachusetts Institute of Technology, *Chair*
THOMAS BERSON, Anagram Laboratories
MARJORY BLUMENTHAL,[1] Georgetown University

Staff

HERBERT S. LIN, Study Director and Chief Scientist, Computer Science and Telecommunications Board
ERIC WHITAKER, Senior Program Assistant, Computer Science and Telecommunications Board

---

[1] Ms. Blumenthal resigned from the committee on May 1, 2013, and accepted a position as executive director for the President's Council of Advisors on Science and Technology.

Preface

Today, cybersecurity is widely viewed as a matter of pressing national importance. Many elements of cyberspace are notoriously vulnerable to an expanding range of attacks by a spectrum of hackers, criminals, terrorists, and state actors. For example, government agencies and private-sector companies both large and small suffer from cyber thefts of sensitive information, cyber vandalism (e.g., defacing of Web sites), and denial-of-service attacks. The nation's critical infrastructure, including the electric power grid, air traffic control system, financial systems, and communication networks, depends extensively on information technology for its operation.

Concerns about the vulnerability of the information technology on which the nation relies have deepened in the security-conscious environment after the September 11, 2001, attacks and in light of increased cyber espionage directed at private companies and government agencies in the United States. National policy makers have become increasingly concerned that adversaries backed by considerable resources will attempt to exploit the cyber vulnerabilities in the critical infrastructure, thereby inflicting substantial harm on the nation. Numerous policy proposals have been advanced, and a number of bills have been introduced in Congress to tackle parts of the cybersecurity challenge.

Although the larger public discourse sometimes treats the topic of cybersecurity as a new one, the Computer Science and Telecommunications Board (CSTB) of the National Research Council has long recognized cybersecurity as a major challenge for public policy.[1] CSTB work in cyber-security over more than two decades (Box P.1) offers a wealth of information on practical measures, technical and nontechnical challenges, and potential policy responses. Produced by the Committee on Developing a Cybersecurity Primer: Leveraging Two Decades of National Academies Work (see Appendix A), the present report draws on past insights developed in this body of work to provide a concise primer on the fundamentals of cybersecurity and the nexus between cybersecurity and public policy (see Box P.2 for the project's statement of task).

This report is based primarily on earlier CSTB work (see Appendix B), and for readability, direct extracts from that work are not set in quotation marks, nor are paraphrases from that work identified as such. However, the report also addresses issues not covered in earlier CSTB work, and the committee acknowledges with gratitude input from William Press (University of Texas at Austin), Tim Gibson (Draper Laboratories), Stefan Savage (University of California, San Diego), and William Sanders (University of Illinois at Urbana-Champaign) on a variety of cybersecurity-related topics in the course of its work.

As a primer, this report presents fundamental concepts and principles that serve as points of departure for understanding specific cybersecurity incidents or proposals to improve security. The specifics of cybersecurity change rapidly, but the fundamental concepts and principles endure, or at least they change much more slowly. These concepts and principles are approximately independent of particular cybersecurity technologies or incidents, although they manifest themselves in a wide variety of different technologies and incidents.

The report's emphasis on fundamental concepts and principles also means that in the interest of brevity, coverage in this primer cannot be comprehensive. For readers who wish to explore particular topics more deeply, the detailed CSTB reports listed in Appendix B provide a substantial resource.

---

[1] The Web page at http://sites.nationalacademies.org/CSTB/CSTB_059144 lists all CSTB reports related to cybersecurity.

BOX P.1 Selected Computer Science and Telecommunications Board Work on Cybersecurity—A Brief Summary of Highlights

The 1991 CSTB report *Computers at Risk* warned that "as computer systems become more prevalent, sophisticated, embedded in physical processes, and interconnected, society becomes more vulnerable to poor system design . . . and attacks on computer systems" and that "the nature and magnitude of computer system problems are changing dramatically" (p. 1). It also lamented that "known techniques are not being used" to increase security.

In 1999, CSTB released *Trust in Cyberspace*, which proposed a research agenda to increase the trustworthiness of information technology (IT), with a special focus on networked information systems. This report went beyond security matters alone, addressing as well other dimensions of trustworthiness such as correctness, reliability, safety, and survivability. Importantly, it also noted that "economic and political context is critical to the successful development and deployment of new technologies" (p. viii).

In 2002, CSTB issued *Cybersecurity Today and Tomorrow: Pay Now or Pay Later*, which reprised recommendations from a decade of CSTB cybersecurity studies. Its preface noted that "it is a sad commentary on the state of the world that what CSTB wrote more than 10 years ago is still timely and relevant. For those who work in computer security, there is a deep frustration that research and recommendations do not seem to translate easily into deployment and utilization" (p. v).

CSTB's 2007 report *Toward a Safer and More Secure Cyberspace* observed that "there is an inadequate understanding of what makes IT systems vulnerable to attack, how best to reduce these vulnerabilities, and how to transfer cybersecurity knowledge to actual practice" (p. vii). It set forth an updated research agenda, sought to inspire the nation to strive for a safer and more secure cyberspace, and focused "substantial attention on the very real challenges of incentives, usability, and embedding advances in cybersecurity into real-world products, practices, and services" (p. xii).

In 2009, CSTB turned its attention to the technical and policy dimensions of cyberattack—the offensive side of cybersecurity. *Technology, Policy, Law, and Ethics Regarding U.S. Acquisition and Use of Cyberattack Capabilities* concluded that although cyberattack capabilities are an important asset for the United States, the current policy and legal framework for their use is ill-formed, undeveloped, and highly uncertain and that U.S. policy should be informed by an open and public national debate on technological, policy, legal, and ethical issues posed by cyberattack capabilities.

In 2010, the CSTB report *Toward Better Usability, Security, and Privacy of Information Technology: Report of a Workshop* identified research opportunities and ways to embed usability considerations in design and development related to security and privacy. In that year, CSTB also produced a second workshop report, *Proceedings of a Workshop on Deterring Cyberattacks: Informing Strategies and Developing Options*, a collection of papers that examined governmental, economic, technical, legal, and psychological challenges involved in deterring cyberattacks.

NOTE: All of these reports were published by the National Academies Press, Washington, D.C.

BOX P.2 The Project Statement of Task

A primer on the technical and policy issues of cybersecurity, building on more than two decades of prior Academies work, will be developed under the auspices of a small study committee. The report will examine what is known about effective technical and nontechnical approaches, the state of the art and open challenges, why relatively little progress has been made in cybersecurity despite the recommendations of many reports from the Academies and elsewhere, and potential policy responses. Much of the material will be drawn directly from previous reports. The committee will also review emerging issues and new technical and nontechnical approaches that may not have been covered in previous National Research Council reports.

Acknowledgment of Reviewers

This report has been reviewed in draft form by individuals chosen for their diverse perspectives and technical expertise, in accordance with procedures approved by the National Research Council's Report Review Committee. The purpose of this independent review is to provide candid and critical comments that will assist the institution in making its published report as sound as possible and to ensure that the report meets institutional standards for objectivity, evidence, and responsiveness to the study charge. The review comments and draft manuscript remain confidential to protect the integrity of the deliberative process. We wish to thank the following individuals for their review of this report:

Steven Bellovin, Columbia University,
RuthAnne Bevier, California Institute of Technology,
Jack Goldsmith, Harvard Law School,
Raymond Jeanloz, University of California, Berkeley,
Anita Jones, University of Virginia,
Butler Lampson, Microsoft Corporation, and
Steven Wallach, Convey Computer Corporation.

Although the reviewers listed above have provided many constructive comments and suggestions, they were not asked to endorse the conclusions, nor did they see the final draft of the report before its release. The review of this report was overseen by Sam Fuller (Analog Devices). Appointed by the National Research Council, he was responsible for making certain that an independent examination of this report was carried out in accordance with institutional procedures and that all review comments were carefully considered. Responsibility for the final content of this report rests entirely with the authoring committee and the institution.

Contents

xiii

Summary

Nations are increasingly dependent on information and information technology. Companies rely on computers for diverse business processes ranging from payroll and accounting to the tracking of inventory and sales, to support for research and development. Distribution of food, water, and energy is dependent on computers and networks at every stage, as is delivery of transportation, health care, and financial services. Modern military forces use weapons that are computer controlled. Even more important, the movements and actions of military forces are increasingly coordinated through computer-based networks that allow information and common pictures of the battlefield to be shared. Logistics are entirely dependent on computer-based scheduling and optimization.

In light of this dependence on information technology, cybersecurity is increasingly important to the nation, and cyberspace is vulnerable to a broad spectrum of hackers, criminals, terrorists, and state actors. Working in cyberspace, these malevolent actors can steal money, intellectual property, or classified information; snoop on private conversations; impersonate law-abiding parties for their own purposes; harass or bully innocent people anonymously; damage important data; destroy or disrupt the operation of physical machinery controlled by computers; or deny the availability of normally accessible services.

A number of factors, such as the September 11, 2001, attacks and higher levels of cyber espionage directed at private companies and government agencies in the United States, have deepened concerns about the vulnerability of the information technology (IT) on which the nation relies. For example, policy makers have become increasingly concerned that adversaries backed by considerable resources will attempt to exploit the cyber vulnerabilities in the critical infrastructure, thereby inflicting substantial harm on the nation. Numerous policy proposals have been advanced, and a number of bills have been introduced in Congress to tackle parts of the cybersecurity challenge.

It is to help decision makers and the interested public make informed choices that this report was assembled. The report is fundamentally a primer on issues at the nexus of public policy and cybersecurity that leverages insights developed in work by the National Research Council's Computer Science and Telecommunications Board over more than two decades on practical measures for cybersecurity, technical and nontechnical challenges, and potential policy responses.

This report defines cyberspace broadly as the artifacts based on or dependent on computing and communications technology; the information that these artifacts use, store, handle, or process; and how these various elements are connected. Security in cyberspace (i.e., cybersecurity) is about technologies, processes, and policies that help to prevent and/or reduce the negative impact of events in cyberspace that can happen as the result of deliberate actions against information technology by a hostile or malevolent actor.

Cybersecurity issues arise because of three factors taken together—the presence of malevolent actors in cyberspace, societal reliance on IT for many important functions, and the inevitable presence of vulnerabilities in IT systems that malevolent actors can take advantage of. Despite these factors, however, we still expect information technologies to do what they are supposed to do and only when they are supposed to do it, and to never do things they are not supposed to do. Fulfilling this expectation is the purpose of cybersecurity.

Against this backdrop, it appears that **cybersecurity is a never-ending battle, and a permanently decisive solution to the problem will not be found in the foreseeable future.**[1] Cybersecurity problems result from the complexity of modern IT systems and human fallibility in making judgments about what actions and information are safe or unsafe from a cybersecurity perspective. Furthermore, threats to cybersecurity evolve, and adversaries—especially at the high-end part of the threat spectrum—constantly adopt new tools and techniques to compromise security when defenses are erected to frustrate them. As information technology becomes more ubiquitously integrated into society, the incentives to compromise the security of deployed IT systems grow. Thus, enhancing the cybersecurity posture of a system—and by extension the organization

---

[1] Text in boldface constitutes the report's findings.

in which it is embedded—must be understood as an ongoing process rather than something that can be done once and then forgotten.

Ultimately, the relevant policy question is not how the cybersecurity problem can be solved, but rather how it can be made manageable. Societal problems related to the existence of war, terrorism, crime, hunger, drug abuse, and so on are rarely "solved" or taken off the policy agenda once and for all. The salience of such problems waxes and wanes, depending on circumstances, and no one expects such problems to be solved so decisively that they will never reappear—and the same is true for cybersecurity.

At the same time, **improvements to the cybersecurity posture of individuals, firms, government agencies, and the nation have considerable value in reducing the loss and damage that may be associated with cybersecurity breaches.** A well-defended target is less attractive to many malevolent actors than are poorly defended targets. In addition, defensive measures force a malevolent actor to expend time and resources to adapt, thus making intrusion attempts slower and more costly and possibly helping to deter future intrusions.

Improvements to cybersecurity call for two distinct kinds of activity: efforts to more effectively and more widely use what is known about improving cybersecurity, and efforts to develop new knowledge about cybersecurity. The gap in security between the U.S. national cybersecurity posture and the threat has two parts. The first part (Part 1) of the gap is the difference between what our cybersecurity posture is and what it could be if known best cybersecurity practices and technologies were widely deployed and used. The second part (Part 2) is the gap between the strongest posture possible with known practices and technologies and the threat as it exists (and will exist). The Part 1 gap is primarily nontechnical in nature (requiring, e.g., research relating to economic or psychological factors regarding the use of known practices and techniques, enhanced educational efforts to promote security-responsible user behavior, and incentives to build organizational cultures with higher degrees of security awareness). Closing the Part 1 gap does not require new technical knowledge of cybersecurity per se, but rather the application of existing technical knowledge. Research will be needed to understand how better to promote deployment and use of such knowledge. Closing the Part 2 gap is where new technologies and approaches are needed, and is the fundamental rationale for technical research in cybersecurity.

Publicly available information and policy actions to date have been insufficient to motivate an adequate sense of urgency and ownership of cybersecurity problems afflicting the United States as a nation. For a number of years, the cybersecurity issue has received increasing public attention, and a greater amount of authoritative information regarding cybersecurity threats is available publicly. But all too many decision makers still focus on the short-term costs of improving their own organizational cybersecurity postures, and little has been done to harness market forces to address matters related to the cybersecurity posture of the nation as a whole. If the nation's cybersecurity posture is to be improved to a level that is higher than the level to which today's market will drive it, the market calculus that motivates organizations to pay attention to cybersecurity must be altered in some fashion.

Cybersecurity is important to the nation, but the United States has other interests as well, some of which conflict with the imperatives of cybersecurity. Tradeoffs are inevitable and will have to be accepted through the nation's political and policy-making processes. Senior policy makers have many issues on their agenda, and they must set priorities for the issues that warrant their attention. In an environment of many competing priorities, reactive policy making is often the outcome. Support for efforts to prevent a disaster that has not yet occurred is typically less than support for efforts to respond to a disaster that has already occurred. In cybersecurity, this tendency is reflected in the notion that "no or few attempts have yet been made to compromise the cybersecurity of application X, and why would anyone want to do so anyway?," thus justifying why immediate attention and action to improve the cybersecurity posture of application X can be deferred or studied further.

Progress in cybersecurity policy has also stalled at least in part because of conflicting equities. As a nation, we want better cybersecurity, yes, but we also want a private sector that innovates rapidly, and the convenience of not having to worry about cybersecurity, and the ability for applications to interoperate easily and quickly with one another, and the right to no diminution in our civil liberties, and so on. Although research and deeper thought may reveal that, in some cases, tradeoffs between security and these other equities are not as stark as they might appear at first glance, policy makers will have to confront rather than elide tensions when they are irreconcilable, and honest acknowledgment and discussion of the tradeoffs (e.g., a better cybersecurity posture may reduce the nation's innovative capability, may increase the inconvenience of using information technology, may reduce the ability to collect intelligence) will go a long way toward building public support for a given policy position.

The use of offensive operations in cyberspace as an instrument to advance U.S. interests raises many important technical, legal, and policy questions that have yet to be aired publicly by the U.S. government. Some of these questions involve topics such as U.S. offensive capabilities in cyberspace, rules of engagement, doctrine for the use of offensive capabilities, organizational responsibilities within the Department of Defense and the intelligence community, and a host of other topics related to offensive operations. It is likely that behind the veil of classification, these topics have been discussed at length. The resulting opacity has many undesirable consequences, but one of the most important consequences is that the role offensive capabilities could play in defending important information technology assets of the United States cannot be discussed fully.

What is sensitive about offensive U.S. capabilities in cyberspace is generally the fact of U.S. interest in a specific technology for cyberattack (rather than the nature of that technology itself); fragile and sensitive operational details that are not specific to the technologies themselves (e.g., the existence of a covert operative in a specific foreign country, a particular vulnerability, a particular operational program); or U.S. knowledge of the capabilities and intentions of specific adversaries. Such information is legitimately classified but is not particularly relevant for a discussion about what U.S. policy should be. That is, unclassified information provides a generally reasonable basis for understanding what can be done and for policy discussions that focus primarily on what should be done.

In summary, cybersecurity is a complex subject whose understanding requires knowledge and expertise from multiple disciplines, including but not limited to computer science and information technology, psychology, economics, organizational behavior, political science, engineering, sociology, decision sciences, international relations, and law. Although technical measures are an important element, cybersecurity is not primarily a technical matter, although it is easy for policy analysts and others to get lost in the technical details. Furthermore, what is known about cybersecurity is often compartmented along disciplinary lines, reducing the insights available from cross-fertilization.

This report emphasizes two central ideas. The cybersecurity problem will never be solved once and for all. Solutions to the problem, limited in scope and longevity though they may be, are at least as much nontechnical as technical in nature.

1

Why Care About Cybersecurity?

1.1 ON THE MEANING AND IMPORTANCE OF CYBERSPACE AND CYBERSECURITY

Most people in modern society encounter computing and communications technologies all day, every day. Offices and stores and factories and street vendors and taxis are filled with computers, even if the computers are not openly visible. People type at the keyboard of computers or tablets and use their smart phones daily. People's personal lives involve computing through social networking, home management, communication with family and friends, and management of personal affairs. The operation of medical devices implanted in human bodies is controlled by embedded (built-in) microprocessors.

A much larger collection of information technology (IT) is instrumental in the day-to-day operations of companies, organizations, and government. Companies large and small rely on computers for diverse business processes ranging from payroll and accounting to the tracking of inventory and sales, to support for research and development (R&D). The distribution of food and energy from producer to retail consumer depends on computers and networks at every stage. Nearly everyone (in everyday society, business, government, and the military services) relies on wireless and wired digital communications systems. IT is used to execute the principal business processes in government and in many of the largest sectors of the economy, including financial services, health care, utilities, transportation, and retail and management services. Indeed, the architecture of today's enterprise IT systems is the very embodiment of the critical business logic in complex enterprises. Today, it is impossible to imagine the Walmarts, the FedExes, the Amazons, and even the "traditional" industries such as manufacturing without IT.

Today and increasingly in the future, computing and communications technologies (collectively, information technologies) are found and will be more likely to be found in places where they are essentially invisible to everyday view: in cars, wallets, clothing, refrigerators, keys, cabinets, watches, doorbells, medicine bottles, walls, paint, structural beams, roads, dishwashers, identification cards, telephones, and medical devices (including some embedded in human beings). These devices will be connected—the so-called Internet of Things. Computing will be embedded in myriad places and objects; even today, computing devices are easily transported in pockets or on wrists. Computing devices will be coupled to multiple sensors and actuators. Computing and communications will be seamless, enabling the tight integration of personal, family, and business systems. Sensors, effectors, and computing will be networked together so that they pass relevant information to one another automatically.

In this emerging era of truly pervasive computing, the ubiquitous integration of computing and communications technologies into common everyday objects enhances their usefulness and makes life easier and more convenient. Understanding context, personal information appliances will make appropriate information available on demand, enabling users to be more productive in both their personal and their professional lives. And, as has been true with previous generations of IT, interconnections among all of these now-smart objects and appliances will multiply their usefulness many times over.

It is in the context of this technology-rich environment that the term "cyberspace" often arises. Although "cyberspace" does not have a single agreed-upon definition,[1] some things can be said about how the term is used in this report. First, cyberspace is not a physical place, although many elements of cyberspace are indeed physical, do have volume and mass, and are located at points in physical space that can be specified in three spatial dimensions. Second, cyberspace includes but is not limited to the Internet—cyberspace also includes computers (some of which are attached to the Internet and some not) and networks (some of which may be part of the Internet and some not). Third, cyberspace includes many intangibles, such as information and software and how different elements of cyberspace are connected to each other.

So a rough definition might be that cyberspace consists of artifacts

---

[1] For example, a Cisco blog post sought to compare 11 different definitions of cyberspace. See Damir Rajnovic, "Cyberspace—What Is It?," Cisco Blogs, July 26, 2012, available at https://blogs.cisco.com/security/cyberspace-what-is-it/.

based on or dependent on computing and communications technology; the information that these artifacts use, store, handle, or process; and the interconnections among these various elements. But the reader should keep in mind that this is a rough and approximate definition and not a precise one.

Given our dependence on cyberspace, we want and need our information technologies to do what they are supposed to do and only when they are supposed to do it. We also want these technologies to not do things they are not supposed to do. And we want these things to be true in the face of deliberately hostile or antisocial actions.

Cybersecurity issues arise because of three factors taken together. First, we live in a world in which there are parties that will act in deliberately hostile or antisocial ways—parties that would do us harm or separate us from our money or violate our privacy or steal our ideas. Second, we rely on IT for a large and growing number of societal functions. Third, IT systems, no matter how well constructed (and many are not as well constructed as the state of the art would allow), inevitably have vulnerabilities that the bad guys can take advantage of.

Thus, a loosely stated definition of cybersecurity is the following: *Security in cyberspace (i.e., cybersecurity) is about technologies, processes, and policies that help to prevent and/or reduce the negative impact of events in cyberspace that can happen as the result of deliberate actions against information technology by a hostile or malevolent actor.*

To go beyond this loosely stated definition of cybersecurity, it is necessary to elaborate on the meaning of "impact," on what makes impact "negative," and on what makes an actor "hostile" or "malevolent."

By definition, an action that changes the functionality of a given information artifact (software or hardware) has impact—Chapter 3 discusses different kinds of impact that are related to cybersecurity. But any given impact can be positive or negative and any actor can be virtuous or malevolent, depending on the perspective of the parties involved—that is, who is a perpetrator and who is a target.

In many cases with which readers of this report are likely to be concerned, the meanings of these terms are both reasonably clear and shared. For example, with respect to the information technology on which law-abiding U.S. citizens and organizational entities rely, what makes an impact negative is that their information technology no longer works as these parties expect it to work. By contrast, if criminals and terrorists are relying on such technologies and it is the U.S. government that takes actions to render their technologies inoperative, the impact would usually be seen as positive.

Similarly, many repressive regimes put into place various mechanisms in cyberspace to monitor communications of dissidents. These regimes may regard as "malevolent actors" those who help dissidents breach the security of these mechanisms and circumvent government monitoring, but others may well regard such parties as virtuous rather than malevolent actors. Compromising the cybersecurity of an Internet-based mechanism for conducting surveillance against such parties has a negative impact from the standpoint of these regimes, but a positive impact for those seeking to open up these regimes.

There are also cases of concern to readers of this report in which the meanings of "negative" and "malevolent" may not be shared. Consider the debate over Internet surveillance by the National Security Agency (NSA) sparked by the revelations of Edward Snowden starting in June 2013. According to news stories on these documents in the *Washington Post* and the *Guardian*, the NSA has engaged in a broad program of electronic surveillance for counterterrorism purposes.[2] Some of the reactions to these revelations have characterized the NSA's actions as having a significant negative impact on the security of the Internet. Others have defended the actions of the NSA as a vital element in U.S. counterterrorism efforts.

Last, the above definition does not limit cybersecurity to technology. Indeed, one of the most important lessons to emerge from cybersecurity experience accumulated over several decades is that nontechnological factors can have an impact on cybersecurity that is at least as great as technology's impact. A full consideration of cybersecurity necessarily entails significant attention to process (how users of information technology actually use it) and policy (how the organizations of which users are a part ask, incentivize, or require their users to behave).

1.2 CYBERSECURITY AND PUBLIC POLICY CONCERNS

Cybersecurity has been an issue of public policy significance for a number of decades. For example, in 1991 the National Research Council wrote in *Computers at Risk:*

> We are at risk. Increasingly, America depends on computers. They control power delivery, communications, aviation, and financial services. They are used to store vital information, from medical records to business plans to criminal records. Although we trust them, they are vulnerable— to the effects of poor design and insufficient quality control, to accident, and perhaps most alarmingly, to deliberate attack. The modern thief can

---

[2] A summary of these major revelations can be found in Dustin Volz, "Everything We Learned from Edward Snowden in 2013," *National Journal,* December 31, 2013, available at http://www.nationaljournal.com/defense/everything-we-learned-from-edward-snowden-in-2013-20131231.

steal more with a computer than with a gun. Tomorrow's terrorist may be able to do more damage with a keyboard than with a bomb. (p. 7)

What is worrisome from a public policy perspective is that the words above, with only a few modifications, could just as easily have been written today. Today, cybersecurity is still a major issue—indeed, its significance has grown as our reliance on IT has increased. Table 1.1 illustrates some of the security consequences of the changes in the information technology environment in the past 20 years.

The IT on which we rely is for the most part created, owned, and operated by the private sector, which means that improving the cybersecurity posture of the nation will require action by relevant elements of the private sector. Nonetheless, many parties believe that the government has an important role in helping to address cybersecurity problems, in much the same way that the government has many responsibilities for national security, law enforcement, and other problems of societal scale.

TABLE 1.1 Potential Security Consequences of More Than Two Decades' Worth of Change in Information Technology (IT)

Change Since 1990	Potential Security Consequence (illustrative, not comprehensive)
Microprocessors, storage devices, communications links, and so on—the raw hardware underlying IT—demonstrate performance that is several orders of magnitude more capable than their counterparts of 20 years ago.	More integration of IT into the functions of daily life means more opportunities for malevolent actors to compromise those functions.
Devices for computing have shifted toward—or at least expanded to include—mobile computing: tablets, pads, smart phones, smart watches, and so on. Desktop and laptop computers are still important to many end users, especially in business environments, but mobile devices are ubiquitous today. Accompanying this change are new business models for providing software to end users—vendor-controlled or vendor-operated app stores are now common. Many corporate employees use their personally owned computing devices for business purposes.	New security approaches are needed to secure battery-operated devices with relatively little computational power. App stores can provide greater assurance about the security of installed software. Enterprises cannot exercise total control over computing resources used on their behalf.

continued

TABLE 1.1 Continued

Change Since 1990	Potential Security Consequence (illustrative, not comprehensive)
Cyberphysical systems are physical systems that are controlled at least in part by IT. Physical devices with embedded computing accept data from the physical world (through sensors such as cameras or thermometers) and/or cause changes in the physical world (through actuators such as a motor that causes something to move or a heater that heats a fluid). Such systems are everywhere—in manufacturing assembly lines, chemical production plants, power generation and transmission facilities, automobiles, airplanes, buildings, heating and cooling facilities, and so on—because IT helps to optimize the use and operation of these systems.	IT-based control of cyberphysical systems means that cybersecurity compromises can affect physical systems and may cause death, destruction, or physical damage.
Cloud computing has become increasingly popular as a way for businesses (and individuals) to increase the efficiency of their IT operations. By centralizing management and IT infrastructure, cloud computing promises to reduce the cost of computing and increase its accessibility to a geographically dispersed user base.	Concentration of computing resources for many parties potentially offers a "big fat target" for malevolent actors. Cloud computing infrastructure may also provide malevolent actors a platform from which to launch their attack. Greater centralization, however, enables providers of computing services to exercise tighter control over security by highly experienced and more expert security-knowledgeable administrators.
The number of Internet users has grown by at least two orders of magnitude in the past two decades, and hundreds of millions of new users (perhaps as many as a billion) will begin to use the Internet as large parts of Africa, South America, and Asia come online in the next decade. Cyberphysical devices will become increasingly connected to the Internet of Things, on the theory that network connections between these devices will enable them to operate more efficiently and effectively.	Inexperienced users are more untutored in the need for security and are thus more vulnerable.

A larger user base means a larger number of potentially malevolent actors. |
| The rise of social networking and computing, as exemplified by applications such as Facebook and Twitter, is based on the ability of IT to bring large numbers of people into contact with one another. | Connectivity among friends and contacts offers opportunities for malevolent actors to improperly take advantage of trust relationships. |

Public policy concerns about the effects of inadequate cybersecurity are often lumped into a number of categories:

- *Cybercrime.* Cybercrime can be broadly characterized as the use of the Internet and IT to steal valuable assets (e.g., money) from their rightful owners or otherwise to take actions that would be regarded as criminal if these actions were taken in person, and a breach of security is usually an important element of the crime. Criminal activity using cyber means includes cyber fraud and theft of services (e.g., stealing credit card numbers); cyber harassment and bullying (e.g., taking advantage of online anonymity to threaten a victim); cyber vandalism (e.g., defacing a Web site); penetration or circumvention of cybersecurity mechanisms intended to protect the privacy of communications or stored information (e.g., tapping a phone call without legal authorization); and impersonation or identity theft (e.g., stealing login names and passwords to forge e-mail or to improperly manipulate bank accounts). Loss of privacy and theft of intellectual property are also crimes (at least sometimes) but generally occupy their own categories of concern. Note also that in addition to the direct financial effects of cybercrime, measures taken to enhance cybersecurity consume resources (e.g., money, talent) that could be better used to build improved products or services or to create new knowledge. And, in some cases, concerns about cybersecurity have been known to inhibit the use of IT for some particular application, thus leading to self-denial of the benefits such an application might bring.
- *Loss of privacy.* Losses of privacy can result from the actions of others or of the individual concerned. Large-scale data breaches occur from time to time, for reasons including loss of laptops containing sensitive data and system penetrations by sophisticated intruders. Intruders have used the sound and video capabilities of home computers for blackmail and extortion. In other cases, individuals post information in their IT-based social networks without understanding the privacy implications of doing so, and are later surprised when such information is accessible to parties that they have not explicitly authorized for such access. Individuals are concerned about the privacy of their data and communications, and a variety of U.S. laws guard against improper disclosure of such information.
- *Activism.* Activism is often defined as nongovernmental efforts to promote, block, or protest social or political change. Compromises in cybersecurity have been used in some activist efforts in cyberspace, wherein activists may compromise the cybersecurity of an installation in an effort to make a political statement or to call attention to a cause, for example, by improperly obtaining classified documents for subsequent release or by defacing a public-facing Web site. Activism may also be an

expression of patriotism, e.g., defacement by citizens of Nation A of Web sites belonging to adversaries of Nation A.

• *Misappropriation of intellectual property* such as proprietary software, R&D work, blueprints, trade secrets, and other product information. Concern over theft of intellectual property is especially pronounced when the targeted firms are part of the defense industrial base and supply key goods and services vital to national security. Although misappropriation of trade secrets is prohibited under international trade law, many countries in the world conduct activities aimed at collecting information that might be economically useful to their domestic companies.[3] Private companies also have incentives to undertake these latter activities, although in many cases some of such activity is forbidden by domestic laws.

• *Espionage.* Espionage refers to one nation's attempts to gather intelligence on other nations, where intelligence information includes information related to national security and foreign affairs. Cyber espionage refers to national-level entities conducting espionage activities using cyber means to obtain important intelligence information relevant to national security (such as classified documents). As a general rule, one nation's collection of intelligence information about another nation is not prohibited under international law.

• *Denials (or disruption) of service.* When services are not available when needed, the elements of society that rely on those services are inconvenienced and may be harmed. Denials of service per se do not necessarily entail actual damage to the facilities providing service. For example, an attacker might flood the telephone network with calls, making it impossible to place one, but as soon as the attacker stops, it again becomes possible to make a call. Denial of services is described further in Chapter 3.

• *Destruction of or damage to physical property.* Such concerns fall into three general categories:

— *Individual cyberphysical systems*, such as automobiles, airliners, and medical devices. Increasingly, computers control the operation of such systems, and communications links, either wired or wireless, connect them to other computational devices. Thus, a malevolent actor might be able to improperly assume control of individual cyberphysical systems or to obtain information (e.g., medical information) that should be private.

— *Critical infrastructure*, which includes multiple facilities for electric power generation and transmission, telecommunications, banking and finance, transportation, oil and gas production and storage, and water supply. Although failures in individual facilities

---

[3] The U.S. government has an explicit policy against conducting such activities.

might be expected from time to time, near-simultaneous failure of multiple facilities might have catastrophic results, such as extensive loss of life, long-lasting disruption of the services that these facilities provide, or significant property damage and economic loss. Policy makers have become increasingly concerned about cyber threats to critical infrastructure emanating from both nations and terrorist groups.

— *Public confidence.* Modern economies depend in large measure on public confidence in the institutions and services that support everyday activities. Under some circumstances, it is possible that even localized damage to some critical part of infrastructure (or even symbols of the nation, such as important monuments) could have a massive effect on public confidence, and thus certain types of attack that would not cause extensive actual damage must be considered to have some catastrophic potential as well.

As far as is known publicly, actual destruction of or damage to physical property to date has been a relatively rare occurrence, although there have been many incidents in the other categories outlined above.

• *Threats to national security and cyber war.* U.S. armed forces depend heavily on IT for virtually every aspect of their capabilities—weapons systems; systems for command, control, communications, and intelligence; systems for managing logistics; and systems for administration. Given that dependence, potential adversaries are developing ways to threaten the IT underlying U.S. military power.[4] In addition, other nations are also using IT in the same ways that the United States is using it, for both military and civilian purposes, suggesting that the United States could itself seek opportunities to advance its national interests by going on the offensive in cyberspace.

Concerns about the areas described above have made cybersecurity a hot topic that has garnered substantial public and government attention. In international circles too, such as the United Nations and NATO, as well as in bilateral relationships with parties such as China and the European Union, cybersecurity is moving higher on the agenda.

But as important as cybersecurity is to the nation, progress in public policy to improve the nation's cybersecurity posture has not been as rapid as might have been expected. One reason—perhaps the most important reason—is that cybersecurity is only one of a number of significant public policy issues—and measures taken to improve cybersecurity potentially

---

[4] See, for example, U.S. Department of Defense, *Department of Defense Strategy for Operating in Cyberspace*, July 2011, available at www.defense.gov/news/d20110714cyber.pdf.

have negative effects in these other areas. Some of the most important conflicts arise with respect to:

- *Economics.* The costs of action to improve cybersecurity beyond an individual organization's immediate needs are high and not obviously necessary, and the costs of inaction are not borne by the relevant decision makers. Decision makers discount future possibilities so much that they do not see the need for present-day action. Also, cybersecurity is increasingly regarded as a part of risk management—an important part in many cases, but nonetheless only a part. And this reality is reflected in policy debates as well—with all of the competing demands for a share of government budgets and attention from senior policy makers, policy progress in cybersecurity has been slower than many have desired.

- *Innovation.* The private sector is constantly trying to bring forward new applications and technologies that improve on old ways of performing certain functions and offer useful new functions. But attention to security can slow bringing new products and services to market, with the result that new technologies and applications are often offered for general use without the benefit of a review for effective security. The public policy question is how to manage the tradeoff between the pace of innovation and a more robust security posture.

- *Civil liberties.* Some measures proposed to improve cybersecurity for the nation potentially infringe on civil liberties, such as privacy, anonymity, due process, freedom of association, free speech, and due process. Advocates of such measures either argue that their favored measures do not infringe on civil liberties, or assert that the infringements are small and relatively insignificant. In some cases, potential infringements arise because changes in information technology have gone beyond the technology base extant when important legal precedents were established. For example, a 1979 Supreme Court case (*Smith* vs. *Maryland*) held that metadata on phone calls (i.e., the phone numbers involved and the duration and time of the call) was less worthy of privacy protection than was "content" information, that is, what the parties to a phone call actually say to each other. But the concept of metadata has come to mean "data associated with a communication that is not communications content," and given the way modern electronic communications operate, the relevance of the 1979 precedent has been challenged as many analysts assert that metadata is *more* revealing than content information.[5]

---

[5] See, for example, Susan Landau, "Highlights from Making Sense of Snowden, Part II: What's Significant in the NSA Revelations," *IEEE Security and Privacy* 12(1, January/February):62-64, 2014, available at http://doi.ieeecomputersociety.org/10.1109/MSP.2013.161. The sense in which metadata is or is not "more" revealing depends on context,

- *International relations and national security.* Because of the world-wide Internet and a global supply chain in which important elements of information technology are created, manufactured, and sold around the world, cyberspace does not have physical national borders. But the world is organized around nation-states and national governments, and every physical artifact of information technology is located *somewhere.* Consequently, one might expect cyberspace-related tensions to arise between nations exercising sovereignty over their national affairs and interacting with other nations—that is, in their international relations.

1.3 ORGANIZATION OF THIS REPORT

Chapter 2 presents some fundamental concepts in information technology that are necessary for understanding cybersecurity. Chapter 3 explores different kinds of cybersecurity threats and actors and explains what it means to compromise cybersecurity. Chapter 4 describes a variety of methods for strengthening and enhancing cybersecurity. Chapter 5 is devoted to a further discussion of key public policy issues relating to cybersecurity. Chapter 6 provides a number of takeaway findings.

---

of course. Large-scale analysis of phone metadata reveals patterns of communication—the identities of communicating parties, and when and with what frequency such communications occur. For some people in some situations, a map of their communications patterns is more privacy-sensitive than what they are saying in their conversations or even in any one conversation; in other situations for other people, their patterns of communication are less sensitive.

2

Some Basics of Computing and Communications Technology and Their Significance for Cybersecurity

2.1 COMPUTING TECHNOLOGY

The computers at the heart of information technology are generally stored-program computers. A program is the way an algorithm is represented in a form understandable by a computer. An algorithm is a particular method devised to solve a particular problem (or class of problems). Computers do what the program tells them to do given particular input data, and if a computer exhibits a particular capability, it is because someone figured out how to break the task into a sequence of basic steps, that is, how to program it.

A program is implemented as a sequence of instructions to the computer; each instruction directs the computer to take some action, such as adding two numbers or activating a device connected to it. Instructions are stored in the memory of the computer, as are the data on which these instructions operate.

A particularly important instruction is conditional. Let's call X a statement about some particular data that is either true or false. Then if X is true, the computer does something (call it A); if X is not true, the computer does something else (call it B). In this way, the sequence of instructions carried out by the computer will differ depending on the exact values of the data provided to the computer. Furthermore, the number of possible sequences of instruction execution grows very rapidly with the number of decisions: a program with only 10 "yes" or "no" decisions can have more than 1000 possible paths, and one with 20 such decisions can have more than 1 million.

A second key point about computing is that information processed by computers and communication systems is represented as sequences of bits (i.e., binary digits). Such a representation is a uniform way for computers and communication systems to store and transmit all information; in principle, information can be synthesized without an original source per se simply by creating the bits and then can be used to produce everything from photo-realistic images to an animation to forged e-mail. Digital encoding can represent many kinds of information with which human beings interact, such as text, sound, images, and video/movies.

As bit sequences, information can be found in two forms—information at rest, that is, stored as a file on a device such as a hard disk or a memory card; and information in transit through a cable or over a wireless link from one location to another.

Why do these aspects of computing technology matter for security?

The fact that a program may execute different instructions in sequence depending on the data means that the programmer must anticipate what the program should do for all possible data inputs. This mental task is of course more difficult when the number of possible different data inputs is large, and many security flaws occur because a programmer has failed to properly anticipate some particular set of data (e.g., the program processes only numeric input, and fails to account for the possibility that a user might input a letter).

A further consequence is that for programs of any meaningful utility, testing for all possible outcomes is essentially impossible when treating the program as a black box and exercising the program by varying the inputs. This means that although it may be possible to show that the program does what it is supposed to do when presented with certain inputs, it is impossible to show that it will never do what it is not supposed to do with all possible inputs. For example, a program may always perform as it should except when one of the inputs is a particular sequence of digits; upon receiving that particular sequence, the program can (deliberately) perform some unexpected and hostile action.

The digital representation of information has a number of important security consequences as well. For example, representation of information as sequences of bits means that there is no inherent association between a given piece of information (whether text, data, or program) and its originator—that is, information is inherently anonymous. A programmer can explicitly record that association as additional encoded data, but that additional data can, in principle, be separated from the information of interest. This point matters in situations in which knowing the association between information and its originator is relevant to security, as might be the case if a law enforcement agency were trying to track down a cyber criminal.

The fact that a given sequence of bits could just as easily be a program as data means that a computer that receives information assuming it to be data could in fact be receiving a program, and that program could be hostile. Mechanisms in a computer are supposed to keep data and program separate, but these mechanisms are not foolproof and can sometimes be tricked into allowing the computer to interpret data as instructions. It is for this reason that downloading data files to a computer can sometimes be harmful to the computer's operation—embedded in those data files can be programs that can penetrate the computer's security, and opening the files may enable such programs to run.

Last, the representation of information as sequences of bits has facilitated the use of various mathematical techniques—cryptographic techniques—to protect such information. Cryptography has many purposes: to ensure the integrity of data (i.e., to ensure that data retrieved or received are identical to data originally stored or sent), to authenticate specific parties (i.e., to verify that the purported sender or author of a message is indeed its real sender or author), and to preserve the confidentiality of information that may have come improperly into the possession of unauthorized parties.

To understand how cryptographic methods span a range of communication and storage needs, consider the general problem of securing a private message sent from Alice to Bob. Years ago, such a process was accomplished by Alice writing a letter containing her signature (authentication). The letter was sealed inside a container to prevent accidental disclosure (confidential transmission). If Bob received the container with an unbroken seal, it meant that the letter had not been disclosed or altered (data integrity), and Bob would verify Alice's signature and read the message. If he received the container with a broken seal, Bob would then take appropriate actions.

With modern cryptographic techniques, each of the steps remains essentially the same, except that automated tools perform most of the work. Mathematical operations can scramble (encrypt) the bit sequences that represent information so that an unauthorized party in possession of them cannot interpret their meaning. Other mathematical operations descramble (decrypt) the scrambled bits so that they can be interpreted properly and the information they represent can be recovered. Still other operations can be used to "sign" a piece of information in a way that associates a particular party with that information. (Note, however, that signed information can always be separated from its signature, and a different signature (and party) can then be associated with that information.)

2.2 COMMUNICATIONS TECHNOLOGY AND THE INTERNET

Computers are frequently connected through networks to communicate with each other, thus magnifying their usefulness. Furthermore, since computers can be embedded in almost any device, arrays of devices can be created that work together for coherent and common purposes.

The most widely known example of a network today is the Internet, which is a diverse set of independent networks, interlinked to provide its users with the appearance of a single, uniform network. That is, the Internet is a network of networks. The networks that compose the Internet share a common architecture (how the components of the networks interrelate) and protocols (standards governing the interchange of data) that enable communication within and among the constituent networks. These networks themselves range in scale from point-to-point links between individual devices (such as Bluetooth) to the relatively small networks operated by individual organizations, to regional Internet service providers, to much larger "backbone" networks that aggregate traffic from many small networks, carry such traffic over long distances, and exchange traffic with other backbone networks.

Internally, the Internet has two types of elements: communication links, channels over which data travel from point to point; and routers, computers at the network's nodes that direct data arriving along incoming links to outgoing links that will take the data toward their destinations.

Data travel along the Internet's communication links in packets adhering to the standard Internet Protocol (IP) that defines the packets' format and header information. Header information includes information such as the origin and destination IP addresses of a packet, which routers use to determine which link to direct the packet along. A message from a sender to a receiver might be broken into multiple packets, each of which might follow a different path through the Internet. Information in the packets' headers enables the message to be restored to its proper order at its destination. However, as a general rule, it is not possible to specify in advance the particular sequence of routers that will handle a given packet—the routers themselves make decisions about where to send a packet in real time, based on a variety of information available to those routers about the cost of transmission to different routers, outages in adjacent routers, and so on.

The origins and destinations of data transiting the Internet are computers (or other digital devices), which are typically connected to the Internet through an Internet service provider (ISP) that handles the necessary technical and administrative arrangements. The links and routers of the Internet provide the critical connectivity among source and destination computers, but nothing else. (Distinguishing between source/

BOX 2.1 A More Refined View of Internet Architecture

The separation of the Internet into nodes for transmitting and receiving data and links and routers for moving data through the Internet captures the essence of its original architectural design, but in truth it presents a somewhat oversimplified picture. Some of the more important adjustments to this picture include the following:

- *Content delivery networks.* Certain popular sites on the Web serve a large number of end users. To increase the speed of delivering content from these sites to end users, these Web sites replicate the most popular content on content delivery networks located across the Internet. When a user requests content from these popular sites, the content is in fact delivered to the user by one of these content delivery networks.
- *Other networks.* As noted in the main text, the Internet is a network of networks. Each network within the Internet is controlled by some entity, such as an Internet service provider, a business enterprise, a government agency, and so on. The controlling entity has relationships with the users to whom it provides service and with the entity controlling the larger network within which this network is embedded. Each relationship is governed by negotiated terms of service. These entities do have capabilities for monitoring traffic and modulating connectivity on their networks, so that, for example, they can cut off certain nodes that are pumping hostile or adverse traffic onto the larger Internet.
- *Cloud computing and storage.* Cloud computing and storage, as well as services such as Internet search, are Internet applications. Various vendors also sell to end users cloud-based services that provide software and even infrastructure on demand. However, from the standpoint of individual users, cloud computing may appear to be located among the links and routers, because the information technology on which such applications run is not co-located with end users.

Misbehavior in any of these components reroutes, delays, or drops traffic inappropriately, or otherwise provides unreliable information, thus posing security risks.

---

destination computers transmitting and receiving data and links and routers moving data through the Internet captures the essence of its original architectural design, but in truth it presents a somewhat oversimplified picture. Some of the more important adjustments to this picture are described in Box 2.1.)

Figure 2.1 provides a schematic that illustrates the architecture of the Internet. Applications that are directly useful to users are provided by the source and destination computers. Applications are connected to each other using packet-switching technology, which runs on the physical infrastructure of the Internet (e.g., fiber-optic cable, wireless data

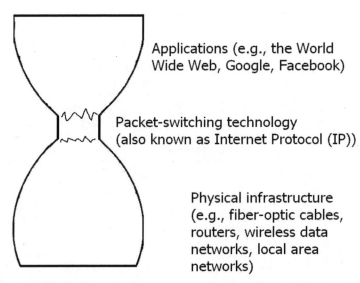

Applications (e.g., the World
Wide Web, Google, Facebook)

Packet-switching technology
(also known as Internet Protocol (IP))

Physical infrastructure
(e.g., fiber-optic cables,
routers, wireless data
networks, local area
networks)

FIGURE 2.1 A schematic of the Internet. Three "layers" of the Internet are depicted. The top and bottom layers (the applications layer and the physical infrastructure layer) are shown as much wider than the middle layer (the packet-switching layer), because within each of the wide layers is found a large number of largely independent actors. But within the packet-switching layer, the number of relevant actors is much smaller, and those that do have some control over the packet-switching layer act in tight coordination.

networks, local area networks). Users navigate the Internet using the arrangements described in Box 2.2.

The various applications, the packet-switching technology, and the physical infrastructure are often called layers of the Internet's architecture, and one of the most significant features of this architecture is that different parties control different layers. Applications (and the infrastructure on which they run) are developed, deployed, and controlled by millions of different entities—companies, individuals, government agencies, and so on. Each of these entities decides what it wants to do, and "puts it on the Internet." The physical infrastructure responsible for carrying packets is also controlled by a diverse group of telecommunications and Internet service providers that are a mix of public and private parties with interests—monetary or otherwise—in being able to carry data packets. (In the United States, these service providers are mostly entities in the private sector.)

The middle layer—the packet technology (in this context essentially

---

BOX 2.2 Internet Navigation

How can a user navigate from one computer to another on the Internet? To navigate—to follow a course to a goal—across any space requires a method for designating locations in that space. On a topographic map, each location is designated by a combination of a latitude and a longitude. In the telephone system, a telephone number corresponding to a landline designates each location. On a street map, locations are designated by street addresses. Just like a physical neighborhood, the Internet has addresses—32- or 128-bit numbers, called IP addresses (IP for Internet Protocol)—that define the specific location of every device on the Internet.

Also like the physical world, the Internet has names—called domain names, which are generally more easily remembered and informative than the addresses that are attached to most devices—that serve as unchanging identifiers of those devices even when their specific addresses are changed. The use of domain names on the Internet relies on a system of servers—called name servers—that translate the user-friendly domain names into the corresponding IP addresses. This system of addresses and names linked by name servers is called the Domain Name System (DNS) and is the basic infrastructure supporting navigation across the Internet.

Conceptually, the DNS is in essence a directory assistance service. George uses directory assistance to look up Sam's number, so that George can call Sam. Similarly, a user who wants to visit the home page of the National Academy of Sciences must either know that the IP address for this page is 144.171.1.30, or use the DNS to perform the lookup for www.nas.edu. The user gives the name www.nas.edu to a DNS name server and receives in return the IP address 144.171.1.30. However, in practice, the user almost never calls on the DNS explicitly—rather, the entire process of DNS lookup is hidden from the user in the process of viewing a Web page, sending e-mail, and so on.

Disruptions to the DNS affect the user experience. Disruptions may prevent users from accessing the Web sites of their choosing. A disruption can lead a user to a "look-alike" Web site pretending to be its legitimate counterpart. If the look-alike site is operated by a malevolent actors, the tricked user may lose control of vital information (such as login credentials).

---

a set of standards for the Internet Protocol discussed above)—is managed and specified by the Internet Engineering Task Force (IETF; Box 2.3). Notably, the IETF and thus the specifications of the Internet Protocol are not under the control of any government, although governments (and many others as well) have input into the processes that evolve the Internet Protocol.

It is the separation of the Internet into different layers that are managed separately that is responsible more than any other factor for the explosive growth of Internet applications and use. By minimizing what

---

BOX 2.3 The Internet Engineering Task Force

The Internet Engineering Task Force (IETF) is a large, open international community of network designers, operators, vendors, and researchers concerned with the evolution of the Internet architecture and the smooth operation of the Internet. It is open to any interested individual. The actual technical work of the IETF is done in its working groups, which are organized by topic into several areas (e.g., routing, transport, security, and so on). Much of the work is handled via mailing lists. The IETF holds meetings three times per year.

The IETF describes its mission as "mak[ing] the Internet work better by producing high quality, relevant technical documents that influence the way people design, use, and manage the Internet." The IETF adheres to a number of principles:

- *Open process.* Any interested person can participate in the work, know what is being decided, and make his or her voice heard on an issue. All IETF documents, mailing lists, attendance lists, and meeting minutes are publicly available on the Internet.
- *Technical competence.* The issues addressed in IETF-produced documents are issues that the IETF has the competence to speak to, and the IETF is willing to listen to technically competent input from any source. The IETF's technical competence also means that IETF output is designed to sound network engineering principles, an element often referred to as "engineering quality."
- *Volunteer core.* IETF participants and leaders are people who come to the IETF because they want to do work that furthers IETF's mission of "making the Internet work better."
- *Rough consensus and running code.* The IETF makes standards based on the combined engineering judgment of its participants and their real-world experience in implementing and deploying its specifications.
- *Protocol ownership.* When the IETF takes ownership of a protocol or function, it accepts the responsibility for all aspects of the protocol, even though some aspects may rarely or never be seen on the Internet. Conversely, when the IETF is not responsible for a protocol or function, it does not attempt to exert control over it, even though such a protocol or function may at times touch or affect the Internet.

SOURCE: Adapted from material found at the IETF Web site at http://www.ietf.org.

---

the links and routers need to do (they only have to transport digitized data from A to B without regard for the content of that data), any given applications provider can architect a service without having to obtain agreement from any other party. As long as the data packets are properly formed and adhere to the standard Internet Protocol, the application provider can be assured that the transport mechanisms will accept the data for forwarding to users of the application. Interpretation of those packets is the responsibility of programs on the receiver's end.

Put differently, most of the service innovation—that is, the applications directly useful to users—takes place at the source and destination computers, independently of the network itself, apart from the technical need for sending and receiving packets that conform to the Internet Protocol. The Internet's architecture is an embodiment of the end-to-end argument in systems design that says that "the network should provide a very basic level of service—data transport—and that the intelligence— the information processing needed to provide applications—should be located in or close to the devices attached to . . . the network."[1] As a result, innovation requires no coordination with network architects or operators, as long as the basic protocols are adhered to. All of the services commonly available on the Internet today—e-mail, the World Wide Web, Facebook, Google search services, voice-over-IP communications services, and so on—have benefited from and been enabled by this architecture.

Why do these aspects of communications technology and the Internet matter for security?

The fundamental architecture of the Internet also has many implications for security. In particular, the end-to-end design philosophy of the Internet is that the Internet should only provide capability for transporting information from one point to another. As such, the Internet's design philosophy makes no special provision for security services. Instead, the Internet operates under the assumption that any properly formed packet found on the network is legitimate; routers forward such packets to the appropriate address—and don't do anything else.

Discussions of cybersecurity for "the Internet" often carry a built-in ambiguity. From the standpoint of most users, "the Internet" refers to all of the layers depicted in Figure 2.1—that is, users' conception of "Internet security" includes the security of the source and destination computers connected to the Internet. From the standpoint of most technologists, however, "the Internet" refers only to the packet-switching technology. This distinction is important because the locus of many cybersecurity problems is found in the applications that use the Internet.

In principle, security mechanisms can be situated at every layer. Depending on the layer, these mechanisms will have different properties and capabilities, and will be implemented by different parties.

Contrary to the Internet's end-to-end design philosophy, some parties argue that the Internet needs security services that are more embedded into the Internet's architecture and protocols and active in the packet-switching layer. These services would be able to monitor Internet traffic for a wide range of security threats, and perhaps take action to curb or

---

[1] See Jerome H. Saltzer, David P. Reed, and David D. Clark, "End-to-End Arguments in System Design," *ACM Transactions on Computer Systems* 2(4):277-288, 1984.

reduce threat-containing traffic and thereby reduce the threat to application users. Further, this argument implies that the end-to-end design philosophy has impeded or even prevented the growth of such security services.

Those favoring the preservation of the end-to-end design philosophy argue that because of the higher potential for inadvertent disruption as a side effect of a change in architecture or protocols, every proposed change must be tested and validated. Because such changes potentially affect an enormous number of users, testing and validation can be difficult and time-consuming—and thus raise concerns about negative impacts on the pace of innovation in new Internet-based products and services. Moreover, actions driven by the requirements of protocols necessarily slow down the speed at which packets can be forwarded to their destinations. And any mechanisms to enforce security mechanisms embedded in Internet protocols may themselves be vulnerable to compromise that may have wide-ranging effects.

Others argue that security services should be the responsibility of the developers of individual applications. In this view, the security functionality provided can be tailored to the needs of the application, and providing security for the application in a decentralized manner does not affect the performance of the Internet as a whole. In addition, the scope and nature of security services provided need not be negotiated with stakeholders responsible for other applications. Countering this viewpoint is the perspective that applications-based security is a burden on end users.

Some security services can be provided at a distance from the applications. For example, some individual ISPs offer their customers (and only their customers) services that help to block hostile traffic or to inform them when they detect that a user's security has been compromised. Such offerings are not uncommon, and they have a modest impact on users' ability to innovate, but they are also generally insufficient to fully mitigate Internet-based threats to cybersecurity. In addition, individual organizations often connect to the Internet using gateways through which flows all the traffic to and from them, and the organizations place services for monitoring and filtering at those gateways.

Whether and how to violate the end-to-end principle in the name of security is an important policy issue today. How this issue is resolved will have profound implications for security.

2.3 INFORMATION TECHNOLOGY SYSTEMS

Information technology (IT) systems integrate computing technology, communication technology, people (such as developers, operators, and users), procedures, and more. Interfaces to other systems and control algorithms are their defining elements; communication and interaction are the currency of their operation. Increasingly, the information exchanged among IT systems includes software (and, therefore, instructions to the systems themselves), often without users knowing what software has entered their systems, let alone what it can do or has done.

The Internet is an essential element of many IT systems—it is the connective tissue that turns a computer 1000 miles away into a component of the IT system with which you interact on your desk or in your hand. For example, Web pages today usually include a pictorial image, which is downloaded from a remote computer onto the displaying computer. But if the portion of the Web browser that displays the image is flawed, and an adversary constructs the image to have a hostile program embedded within it, displaying the image can run the program. Running a Web browser without such a flaw would result in a harmless display of the image.

The security implications of the systems nature of much of the information technology in our lives are addressed further in Chapter 3.

Why do these properties of IT systems matter for security?

Large IT systems—and most of the IT systems that underpin critical infrastructure and daily life alike are large systems—are not simply larger versions of small computer programs. With respect to their cybersecurity properties, they exhibit what might be called emergent behavior—behavior that is rooted in how and when such a system's various components interact with each other.

That is, even an IT system constructed from components that are themselves entirely trustworthy is not necessarily secure. (And, as a general rule, the actual security properties of the components themselves also cannot be assured.) A secure component may be, for example, a program that has been formally proved to meet its specification. But this proof is valid only for the program as a whole. If another component can gain entry to this program in some unanticipated way (e.g., in the middle of the program), the proof may no longer apply.

3

On the Nature of Cybersecurity

Chapter 1 points out that bad things that can happen in cyberspace fall into a number of different categories: cybercrime; losses of privacy; misappropriation of intellectual property such as proprietary software, R&D work, blueprints, trade secrets, and other product information; espionage; disruption of services; destruction of or damage to physical property; and threats to national security. After a brief note about terminology, this chapter addresses how adversarial cyber operations can result in any or all of these outcomes.

3.1 ON THE TERMINOLOGY FOR DISCUSSIONS OF CYBERSECURITY AND PUBLIC POLICY

In developing this report, the committee was faced with an unfortunate lexical reality—there is no consistent or uniform vocabulary (never mind the conceptual basis) for discussions about cybersecurity and public policy. One might expect this to be true across international borders, where it is well known that translations among English, Chinese, German, Russian, Arabic, French, and Hebrew can be problematic. But it is also the case that even within the United States, different communities—and even different individuals within those communities—use terminology whose definitions and usage conventions are somewhat different.

Perhaps it is not entirely surprising that such variation exists. Concerns about cybersecurity have spread rapidly in the past 10 years to many communities, and a uniform lexical or conceptual structure is unlikely to be established under such circumstances. Further, different vocabularies and concepts often reflect differences in intellectual or mission emphasis and orientation that might differentiate various communities.

As an illustration, consider the term "cyberattack." The term has been used variously to include:

- Any hostile or unfriendly action taken against a computer system or network regardless of purpose or outcome.
- Any hostile or unfriendly action taken against a computer system or network if (and only if) that action is intended to cause a denial of service (discussed below) or damage to or destruction of information stored in or transiting through that system or network. Data exfiltration is not included in this usage. (This particular distinction—between data exfiltration (the essential characteristic of cyber espionage) and other kinds of unfriendly action—has great significance in the context of international law and domestic legal authorities for conducting such actions; these points are discussed further in Section 4.2.3 on domestic and international law.)
- Any hostile or unfriendly action taken against a computer system or network if (and only if) that action is intended to cause damage to or destruction of information stored in or transiting through that system or network *and* is effected primarily through the direct use of information technology. (This definition rules out the use of sledgehammers against a computer or backhoes against fiber-optic cables, although of course such actions can seriously disrupt services provided by the attacked computer or cables.)

Another frequent confusion in the literature or in discussions involves the terms "exploit" and "exploitation." As described below, an exploitation is an attempt to compromise the confidentiality of data, usually by making a copy of it and conveying that copy into an adversary's hands. By contrast, an exploit (that is, "exploit" as a noun) is a mechanism used by an adversary to take advantage of a vulnerability. "Exploit" as a verb (as in "an adversary can exploit vulnerability X) means "to take advantage of" (as in "an adversary can take advantage of vulnerability X").

The reader is cautioned that there are many terms in cybersecurity discussions with related but different definitions: some such terms include "compromise," "penetration," "breach," "intrusion," "exploit," "attack," and "hack." It would be highly desirable for all discussants to standardize on some particular vocabulary, but until that day comes, participants in dialogs about cybersecurity will have to rely on context or otherwise take special care to ensure that they understand a speaker's or writer's intent when certain terms are used.

3.2 WHAT IT MEANS TO BE AN ADVERSARY IN CYBERSPACE

In this report, an adversarial (or hostile) cyber operation is one or more unfriendly actions that are taken by an adversary (or equivalently, an intruder) against a computer system or network for the ultimate purpose of conducting a cyber exploitation or a cyberattack. ("Offensive cyber operations" or "offensive operations in cyberspace" are roughly equivalent from an action standpoint but are terms for operations conducted by the good guys, however the good guys may be defined.) "Cyber incident" can be used more or less interchangeably with "hostile cyber operation," but in this report will usually refer to an adversarial cyber operation conducted sometime in the past.

A hostile or adversarial cyber operation can be an exploitation or an attack.

3.2.1 Cyber Exploitation

A cyber exploitation is an action intended to exfiltrate digitally stored information that should be kept away from unauthorized parties that should not have access to it. To date, the vast majority—nearly all—of actual cyber incidents have been exploitations, and sensitive digitally stored information such as Social Security numbers, medical records, blueprints and other intellectual property, classified information, contract and bid information, and software source code have all been obtained by unauthorized parties.

Exploitations are usually undertaken surreptitiously. The surreptitious nature of an exploitation is one of its key features—a surreptitious exploitation of, say, an individual credit card number is much more effective than a discovered exploitation, because if the exploitation is discovered, the credit card owner can notify the bank and prevent the card's further use.

One of the largest cyber exploitations ever discovered happened in the winter holiday season of 2013, when the Target retail store chain suffered a data breach in which personal information belonging to 70 million to 110 million people was stolen.[1] Such information included names, mailing and e-mail addresses, phone numbers, and credit card numbers. Shortly after the breach occurred, observers noted an order-of-magnitude increase in the number of high-value stolen cards on black market Web sites, from nearly every bank and credit union. The Target

---

[1] Elizabeth A. Harris and Nicole Perlroth, "For Target, the Breach Numbers Grow," *New York Times*, January 10, 2014, available at http://www.nytimes.com/2014/01/11/business/target-breach-affected-70-million-customers.html.

Corporation reported a 46 percent drop in income in the fiscal quarter ending February 1, 2014, relative to the comparable period a year earlier, and it incurred $61 million in breach-related expenses (of which insurance covered 72 percent).[2] Financial institutions spent $200 million to replace credit cards after the breach.[3]

Although the vast majority of cyber exploitations target information stored on a computer or network, they can also seek information in the physical vicinity of a computer when the computer has audio and/or video capabilities. In such cases, an intruder can penetrate the computer and activate the on-board camera or microphone without the knowledge of the user, and thus surreptitiously see what is in front of the camera and hear what is going on nearby. For example, in an August 2013 incident, an extortionist assumed control of the Webcam in the personal computer of the new Miss Teen USA and took pictures that he subsequently used to blackmail the victim.[4] In this incident, the extortionist was able to prevent the warning light on the camera from turning on.

3.2.2 Cyberattack

A cyberattack is an action intended to cause a denial of service or damage to or destruction of information stored in or transiting through an information technology system or network.

A denial-of-service (DOS) attack is intended to render a properly functioning system or network unavailable for normal use. A DOS attack may mean that the e-mail does not go through, or the computer simply freezes, or the response time becomes intolerably long (possibly leading to tangible destruction if, for example, a physical process is being controlled by the system). As a rule, the effects of a DOS attack vanish when the attack ceases. DOS attacks are not uncommon, and have occurred against individual corporations, government agencies (both civilian and military), and nations.

Typically, a DOS attack works by flooding a specific target with bogus requests for service (e.g., requests to display a Web page, to receive and store an e-mail), thereby exhausting the resources available to the target

---

[2] Paul Ziobro, "Target Earnings Suffer After Breach," *Wall Street Journal*, February 27, 2014, available at http://online.wsj.com/news/articles/SB2000142405270230425560457940 6694182132568.

[3] Saabira Chaudhuri, "Cost of Replacing Credit Cards After Target Breach Estimated at $200 Million," *Wall Street Journal*, February 19, 2014, available at http://online.wsj.com/ news/articles/SB10001424052702304675504579391080333769014.

[4] Nate Anderson, "Webcam Spying Goes Mainstream as Miss Teen USA Describes Hack," *Ars Technica*, April 16, 2013, available at http://arstechnica.com/tech-policy/2013/08/ webcam-spying-goes-mainstream-as-miss-teen-usa-describes-hack/.

to handle legitimate requests for service and thus blocking others from using those resources. Such an attack is relatively easy to block if these bogus requests for service come from a single source, because the target can simply drop all service requests from that source. A *distributed* denial-of-service attack can flood the target with multiple requests from many different machines. Since each of these different machines might, in principle, be a legitimate requester of service, dropping all of them runs a higher risk of denying service to legitimate parties. Botnets—a collection of victimized computers that are remotely controlled by an adversary— are often used to conduct DOS attacks (Box 3.1).

A well-known example of a DOS attack occurred on April 27, 2007, when a series of distributed denial-of-service (DDOS) attacks began on a range of Estonian government Web sites, media sites, and online banking services.[5] Attacks were largely conducted using botnets to create network traffic, with the botnets being composed of compromised computers from the United States, Europe, Canada, Brazil, Vietnam, and other countries around the world. The duration and intensity of attacks varied across the Web sites attacked; most attacks lasted 1 minute to 1 hour, and a few lasted up to 10 hours.[6] Attacks were stopped when the attackers ceased their efforts rather than being stopped by Estonian defensive measures.[7] The Estonian government was quick to claim links between those conducting the attacks and the Russian government,[8] although Russian officials denied any involvement.[9]

A damaging or destructive attack can alter a computer's programming in such a way that the computer does not later behave as it should. If a physical device (such as a generator) is controlled by the computer, the operation of that device may be compromised. The attack may also alter or erase digitized data, either stored or in transit (i.e., while it is being sent from one point to another). Such an attack may delete data files irretrievably.

Although the preparation for an attack may be surreptitious (so that

---

[5] *Economist*, "A Cyber-Riot," May 10, 2007; Jaak Aaviksoo, Minister of Defense of Estonia, presentation to Centre for Strategic and International Studies, November 28, 2007.

[6] The most detailed measurements on the attacks are from Arbor Networks. See Jose Nazario, "Estonian DDoS Attacks—A Summary to Date," May 17, 2007, available at http://asert.arbornetworks.com/2007/05/estonian-ddos-attacks-a-summary-to-date/.

[7] McAfee Corporation, *Cybercrime: The Next Wave*, McAfee Virtual Criminology Report, 2007, p. 11, available at http://infovilag.hu/data/files/129623393.pdf.

[8] Maria Danilova, "Anti-Estonia Protests Escalate in Moscow," *Washington Post*, May 2, 2007, available at http://www.washingtonpost.com/wp-dyn/content/article/2007/05/02/AR2007050200671_2.html. The article quotes both the Estonian president and the Estonian ambassador to Russia as claiming Kremlin involvement.

[9] McAfee Corporation, *Cybercrime: The Next Wave*, 2007, p. 7.

BOX 3.1 Botnets

An attack technology of particular power and significance is the botnet. Botnets are collections of victimized computers that are remotely controlled by the attacker. A victimized computer—an individual bot—is connected to the Internet, usually with an "always-on" broadband connection, and is running software clandestinely introduced by the attacker. The attack value of a botnet arises from the sheer number of computers that an attacker can control—often tens or hundreds of thousands and perhaps as many as a million. (An individual unprotected computer may be part of multiple botnets.)

Since all of these computers are under one party's control, the botnet can act as a powerful amplifier of an adversary's actions. In addition, by acting through a botnet, a malevolent actor can be more anonymous (because his actions can be routed through many computers belonging to third parties). The use of botnets can also help to defeat defensive techniques that identify certain computers as sources of hostile traffic—as one bot in the net is identified as a source of hostile traffic, the adversary simply shifts to a second, and a third, and a fourth bot.

An attacker usually builds a botnet by finding a few individual computers to compromise, perhaps using one of the tools described above. The first hostile action that these initial zombies take is to find other machines to compromise—a task that can be undertaken in an automatic manner, and so the size of the botnet can grow quite rapidly.

A botnet controller can communicate with its botnet and still stay in the background, unidentified and far away from any action, while the individual bots—which may belong mostly to innocent parties that may be located anywhere in the world— are the ones that are visible to the party under attack. The botnet controller has great flexibility in the actions it may take—it may direct all of the bots to take the same action, or each of them to take different actions.

Individual bots can probe their immediate environment and take action based on the results of that probe. A bot can pass information it finds back to its controller, or it can take destructive action, which may be triggered at a certain time, or perhaps when the resident bot receives a subsequent communication from the controller. Bots can also obtain new programming from their controllers, giving them great flexibility with respect to the range of harmful tasks they can conduct at any time.

Perhaps the most important point about botnets is the great flexibility they offer to a malevolent actor. Adversaries can obtain botnet services on the open (black) market for hacking services (e.g., the botnets used to attack Estonia in 2007 were apparently rented).[1] Although botnets are known to be well suited to distributed denial-of-service attacks, it is safe to say that their full range of utility for adversarial operations in cyberspace has not yet been examined.

---

[1] Mark Landler and John Markoff, "Digital Fears Emerge After Data Siege in Estonia," *New York Times*, May 29, 2007, available at http://www.nytimes.com/2007/05/29/technology/29estonia.html?pagewanted=all&_r=0.

the victim does not have a chance to prepare for it), the effects of an attack may or may not be concealed. If the intent of an attack is to destroy a generator, an explosion in the generator is obvious (although it may not be traceable to a cyberattack on the controlling computer). But if the intent of an attack is to corrupt vital data, small amounts of corruption may not be visible (and small amounts of corruption continued over time could result in undetectable large-scale corruption).

The best known example of a destructive cyberattack is Stuxnet, a hostile cyber operation that targeted the computer-controlled centrifuges of the uranium enrichment facility in Natanz, Iran.[10] After taking control of these centrifuges, Stuxnet issued instructions to them to operate in ways that would cause them to self-destruct, unbeknownst to the Iranian centrifuge operators.

3.2.3 An Important Commonality for Exploitation and Attack

An important point about cyber exploitation and cyberattack is that they generally use the same basic technical approaches to penetrate the security of a system or network, even though they have different outcomes. (By definition, the former results in exfiltration of data, whereas the latter results in damage to information or information technology—and whatever else that technology controls.) The reason for this similarity is addressed below in Section 3.4. Also, a single offensive operation can, in principle, involve both an exploitation phase and an attack phase.

3.3 INHERENT VULNERABILITIES OF INFORMATION TECHNOLOGY

Designing a completely secure, totally unhackable computer is easy— put the computer into a sealed metal box, with no holes in the box for wires and no way to pass information (recognizing that computer programs are also a form of information) outside the box, and the computer system is entirely secure (see the left side of Figure 3.1). Of course, this system—inside the box—is entirely useless as well. Only by removing the box (which serves as an information barrier) can the computer be made useful (right side of Figure 3.1).

A computer can produce useful results only when it is provided with "correct" or "good" information. But what counts as "good" and "bad" information depends on decisions made by fallible human beings—and in particular humans who may be tricked into believing that certain

---

[10] David Kushner, "The Real Story of Stuxnet," *IEEE Spectrum*, February 26, 2013, available at http://spectrum.ieee.org/telecom/security/the-real-story-of-stuxnet#.

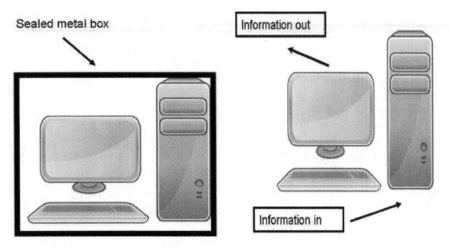

FIGURE 3.1 A secure but useless computer (*left*), and an insecure but useful computer (*right*).

information or programs are good when they are in fact bad. This fact underscores a basic point about most adversarial cyber operations—the key role played by deception. Box 3.2 provides a simple example.

Two other factors compound the inherent vulnerabilities of information technology. First, the costs of an adversarial cyber operation are usually small compared with the costs of defending against it. This asymmetry arises because the victim (the defender) must succeed every time the intruder acts (and may even have to take defensive action long after the intruder's initial penetration if the intruder has left behind an implant for a future attack). By contrast, the intruder needs to succeed in his efforts only once, and if he pays no penalty for a failed operation, he can continue his efforts until he succeeds or chooses to stop.[11]

Second, modern information technology systems are complex entities whose proper (secure) operation requires many actors to have behaved correctly and appropriately and to continue to do so in the future. Each of these actors exerts some control over some aspect of a user's experience or the configuration or functioning of some part of the system, and a problem in any of them can negatively compromise that experience.

As an example, consider the "simple" task of viewing a Web page—

---

[11] This asymmetry applies primarily when the intruder can choose when to act, that is, when the precise timing of the intrusion's success does not matter. If the intruder must succeed on a particular timetable, the intruder does not have an infinitely large number of tries to succeed, and the asymmetry between intruder and defender may be reduced significantly.

BOX 3.2 A Simple Example of Deception

HTML (an acronym for Hypertext Markup Language) is a computer language that is used to display Web pages. One feature of this language is that it enables the conversion of text into links to other Web pages. The user sees on the page a certain text string, but the text string conceals a link—clicking on the "click here" text brings the user to the Web site corresponding to the link. (Although the link can be revealed if the user's pointing device hovers over the text string, many users do not perform such a check.)

But there are no limits on the text string to be displayed to the user, and so it is possible for the user to see on the screen "www.example.com," but underneath the text is really the link for another Web page, such as www.hackyourcomputer. com. Clicking on the text displayed on the screen takes the user to the bad site rather than the intended site.

---

something that many people do every day with ease. The user can type the name of a Web page (called a URL, uniform resource locator) as depicted in the top of Figure 3.2, and the proper Web page appears in a second or two as depicted at the bottom of Figure 3.2. In addition, the user also wants the display of the Web page to be the *only* thing that happens in response to his request—exfiltrating the user's credit card numbers to a cyber criminal or destroying the files on the computer's hard disk are things that the user does not want to happen.

Behind this apparent simplicity is a multitude of steps, as depicted in Figure 3.3. What is immediately clear even without a detailed explanation is that the process involves many actors, and a flawed performance by any of these actors may mean that the requested page does not appear as required.

Inspection of Figure 3.3 with a powerful magnifying lens (not supplied with this report) would reveal that it could be simplified to some extent by considering the display as the result of three interacting parts: preparation of the computer used to display the page, preparation of the Web page that is to be displayed, and the actual retrieval of the Web page from where it is hosted to where it is displayed. Each of these parts is itself composed of actions involving a number of actors. Some of the actors shown in Figure 3.3 include:

- The provider of the hardware and the operating system;
- The delivery service that handles the computer in transit (e.g., UPS/FedEx), which must deliver the box containing the computer from

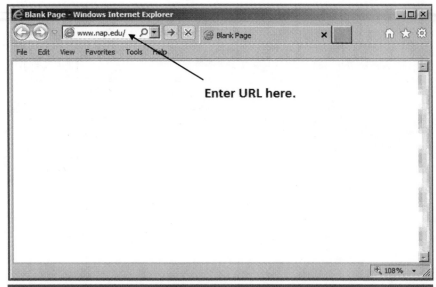

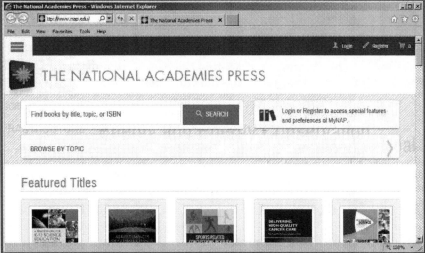

FIGURE 3.2 Viewing a Web page, from the user's perspective. When a user types a Web page's name (*top*), the corresponding page appears and can be read (*bottom*).

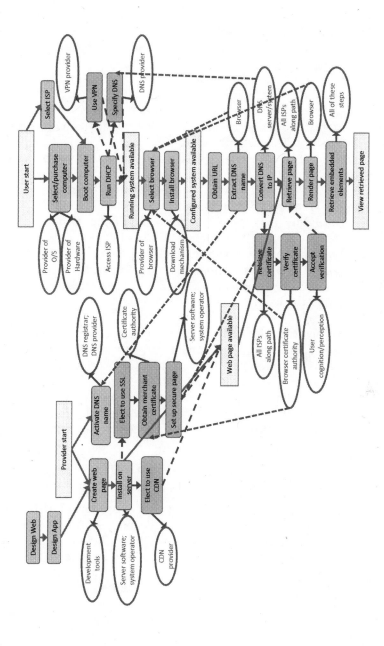

FIGURE 3.3 Viewing a Web page, behind the scenes. SOURCE: David Clark, "Control Point Analysis," ECIR Working Paper, 2012, Telecommunications Policy Research Conference, available at http://ecir.mit.edu/index.php/research/working-papers/278-control-point-analysis. Reprinted by permission.

the factory to the proper destination without allowing an adversary to tamper with it;

• The Internet service provider that provides Internet service to the location where the user accesses the Web page;

• The party responsible for the Internet browser that the user runs to access the Web page;

• The party or parties responsible for various add-ons that the browser runs (e.g., to display PDF files);

• The developer of the tools for creating Web pages;

• The operator of the server that hosts the Web page to be accessed;

• The provider of software for the host server;

• Providers of the advertisement(s) that might be served up along with the Web page;

• The Domain Name System registrar that registers the name of the Web site where the Web page can be found;

• The DNS provider that translates the name of the Web site to a numerical Internet Protocol address such as 144.171.1.4;

• The certificate authority who attests that the purported operator of the Web site is in fact the properly registered operator; and

• All of the Internet service providers along the connection path between the host and the user.

Each of these actors must carry out correctly the role it plays in the overall process; for example, ISPs must correctly operate the routing protocols if packets are to reach their destination. Moreover, each of these actors could take (or be tricked into taking) one or more actions that thwart the user's intent in retrieving a given Web page, which is to receive the requested Web page promptly and to have only that task be accomplished, and not have any other unrequested task be accomplished.

3.4 THE ANATOMY OF ADVERSARIAL ACTIVITIES IN CYBERSPACE

Adversarial operations in cyberspace against a system or network usually require penetration of the system or network's security to deliver a payload that takes action in accordance with the intruder's wishes against the target of interest (e.g., against any of the entities shown in ovals in Figure 3.3). The payload is usually computer code, and is also known as malware. (In some cases, the payload could be instructions or commands issued to the computer by a malevolent actor.)

In a noncyber context, an intruder might penetrate a file cabinet. To penetrate the file cabinet, the intruder must first gain access to it—access to a file cabinet located on the International Space Station would pose a problem very different from that posed by the same cabinet located in an office in Washington, D.C. Once standing in front of the file cabinet, the intruder might take advantage of an easily pickable lock on the cabinet—that is, an easily pickable lock is a vulnerability. The payload in this noncyber context reflects the action taken by the intruder after the lock is picked. For example, the intruder can alter some of the information on those papers, perhaps by replacing certain pages with pages of the intruder's creation (i.e., he alters the data recorded on the pages), he can pour ink over the papers (i.e., he renders the data unavailable to any legitimate user), or he can copy the papers and take the copies away, leaving behind the originals (that is, he exfiltrates the data on the papers).

3.4.1 Cyber Penetration

Access

In a cyber context, an intruder must first penetrate the system or network of interest. The first step is gaining access—an "easy" target is one that the intruder need spend only a little effort preparing and the intruder can gain access to the target without much difficulty, such as a target that is known to be connected to the Internet. Public Web sites are examples of such targets, as they must—by definition—be connected to the Internet to be useful.

Hard targets are those that require a great deal of preparation on the part of the intruder and where access to the target can be gained only at great effort or may even be impossible for all practical purposes. For example, the avionics of a fighter plane are not likely to be directly connected to the Internet for the foreseeable future, which means that launching a cyberattack against such a plane will require some kind of harder-to-achieve access to introduce a vulnerability that can be used later. As a general rule, sensitive and important computer systems or networks are likely to fall into the category of hard targets.

Access paths to a target include those in the following categories:

• *Remote access*, in which the intruder is at some distance from the adversary computer or network of interest. The canonical example of remote access is that of an adversary computer attacked through the access path provided by the Internet, but other examples might include accessing an adversary computer through a dial-up modem attached to it or through penetration of the wireless network to which it is connected. Malevolent actors are constantly searching for new computers on the Internet. When they find one, they are often able to penetrate the computer, and in some cases, such penetration takes only a matter of minutes or hours from the moment of initial connection to the Internet, even without its owner taking any other action at all.[12]

An example of remote access is the use of SQL injection techniques to execute database commands selected by the intruder. Many public-facing Web sites allow a user to enter data through a keyboard. SQL is a common computer language used for managing data input and data manipulation in certain databases. If the SQL coding for managing data input from a user is flawed, it is sometimes possible for the user (the hostile user!) to insert ("inject") database commands of his own into the input. In a 2009 event, the RockYou company, which developed applications for use on social networking sites, suffered an SQL penetration that resulted in making 32 million user names and passwords available to intruders.[13] In 2012, RockYou paid $250,000 in penalties following a settlement with the Federal Trade Commission.[14]

- *Close access*, in which the penetration of a system or network takes place through the local installation of hardware or software functionality by seemingly friendly parties (e.g., covert agents, vendors) in close proximity to the computer or network of interest. Close access is a possibility anywhere in the supply chain of a system that will be deployed (Box 3.3). As a general rule, close access is more expensive, riskier, and harder to conduct than remote access.

One example of a supply chain attack occurred in 2008. According to *The Telegraph*, criminal gangs in China gained access to the supply chain for a certain line of chip-and-pin credit card readers.[15] The gangs modified these readers to surreptitiously relay customer account information (including the security personal identification numbers) to criminal enterprises. The readers were repackaged with virtually no physical traces of tampering and shipped directly to several European countries. Details collected from the cards were used to make duplicate credit cards,

---

[12] See, for example, *Survival Time*, available at http://isc.sans.org/survivaltime.html. Also, in a 2008 experiment conducted in Auckland, New Zealand, an unprotected computer was rendered unusable through online attacks. The computer was probed within 30 seconds of its going online, and the first attempt at intrusion occurred within the first 2 minutes. After 100 minutes, the computer was unusable. See "Experiment Highlights Computer Risks," December 2, 2008, available at http://www.stuff.co.nz/print/4778864a28.html.

[13] Angela Moscaritolo, "RockYou Hack Compromises 32 Million Passwords," *SC Magazine*, December 15, 2009, available at http://www.scmagazine.com/rockyou-hack-compromises-32-million-passwords/article/159676/.

[14] Dan Kaplan, "RockYou to Pay FTC $250K After Breach of 32M Passwords," *SC Magazine*, March 27, 2012, available at http://www.scmagazine.com/rockyou-to-pay-ftc-250k-after-breach-of-32m-passwords/article/233992/.

[15] Henry Samuel, "Chip and Pin Scam 'Has Netted Millions from British Shoppers,'" *The Telegraph*, October 10, 2008, available at http://www.telegraph.co.uk/news/uknews/law-and-order/3173346/Chip-and-pin-scam-has-netted-millions-from-British-shoppers.html.

**BOX 3.3 Close Access Through the
Information Technology Supply Chain**

Systems (and their components) can be penetrated in design, development, testing, production, distribution, installation, configuration, maintenance, and operation. In most cases, the supply chain is only loosely managed, which means that the party supplying the system to the end user may well not have full control over the entire chain. Examples of possible supply-chain penetrations include the following:

• A vendor with an employee loyal to an adversary introduces malicious hardware or code at the factory as part of a system component for which the vendor is a subcontractor in a critical system.

• An adversary intercepts a set of USB flash drives ordered by the victim for distribution at a conference and substitutes a different doctored set for actual delivery to the victims. In addition to the conference proceedings, the adversary places hostile software on the flash drives that the victims install when they plug in the drives.

• An adversary writes an application for a smart device that performs some useful function (e.g., an app that displays a clock on the device's face) but also includes malware that sends the contact list on the device to the adversary.

• An adversary bribes a shipping clerk to look the other way when the computer is on the loading dock for transport to the victim, opens the box, replaces the video card installed by the vendor with one modified by the intruder, and reseals the box.

A supply chain penetration may be effected late in the chain, for example, against a deployed computer in operation or one that is awaiting delivery on a loading dock. In these cases, such a penetration is by its nature narrowly and specifically targeted, and it is also not scalable, because the number of computers that can be penetrated is proportional to the number of human assets available. In other cases, a supply chain penetration may be effected early in the supply chain (e.g., introducing a vulnerability during development), and high leverage against many different targets might result from such an attack.

---

which could then be used for normal financial transactions. MasterCard International estimated that thousands of customer accounts were compromised, netting millions of dollars in ill-gotten gains before the breach was discovered.

• *Social access.* An intruder can gain access by taking advantage of existing trust relationships between people—one is usually more likely to trust the intentions of a known and/or friendly party than an unknown one. Pretending to be a friend or colleague of the victim is one example of the fact that the human beings who install, configure, operate, and use IT systems of interest can often be compromised through recruitment, bribery, blackmail, deception, trickery, or extortion, and these individuals can be of enormous value to the intruder. In some cases, a trusted insider "goes bad" for his or her own reasons and by virtue of the trust placed in him is able to take advantage of his own credentials for improper purposes—this is the classical "insider threat." Social engineering is the use of deception and trickery for gaining access. Social engineering results in the intruder gaining access to the credentials and therefore the access privileges of those the intruder has tricked.

As an example of an adversary taking advantage of social access to penetrate the security of computer systems, consider the case of Edward Snowden, who in June 2013 leaked to the news media classified documents from the National Security Agency and other government agencies in the United States and abroad that described electronic surveillance activities of these agencies around the world. Given the highly classified nature of these documents, many have asked how their security could have been compromised. According to a Reuters news report,[16] Snowden was able to persuade two dozen fellow workers at the NSA to provide him with their credentials, telling them that he needed that information in his role as systems administrator.

Sometimes, social engineering is combined with either remote access or close access methods. An intruder may make contact through the Internet with someone likely to have privileges on the system or network of interest. Through that contact, the intruder can trick the person into taking some action that grants the intruder access to the target. For example, the intruder sends the victim an e-mail with a link to a Web page and when the victim clicks on that link, the Web page may take advantage of a technical vulnerability in the browser to run a hostile program of its own choosing on the user's computer, often or usually without the permission or even the knowledge of the user.

Social engineering can be combined with close access techniques in other ways as well. For example, users can sometimes be tricked or persuaded into inserting hostile USB flash drives into the USB ports of their computer. Because some systems support an "auto-run" feature for insertable media (i.e., when the medium is inserted, the system automatically runs a program named "autorun.exe" on the medium) and the feature is often turned on, a potentially hostile program is executed. Open USB ports can be glued shut, but such a countermeasure also makes it impos-

---

[16] Mark Hosenball and Warren Strobel, "Snowden Persuaded Other NSA Workers to Give Up Passwords–Sources," *Reuters*, November 7, 2013, available at http://www.reuters.com/article/2013/11/08/net-us-usa-security-snowden-idUSBRE9A703020131108.

sible to use the USB ports for *any* purpose. In one experiment, a red team used inexpensive USB flash drives to penetrate an organization's security. The red team scattered USB drives in parking lots, smoking areas, and other areas of high traffic. A program on the USB drive would run if the drive was inserted, and the result was that 75 percent of the USB drives distributed were inserted into a computer.[17]

Vulnerability

Access is only one aspect of a penetration, which also requires the intruder to take advantage of a vulnerability in the target system or network. Examples of vulnerability include an accidentally introduced design or implementation flaw (common), an intentionally introduced design or implementation flaw (less common), or a configuration error in the target such as a default setting that leaves system protections turned off. Vulnerabilities arise from the characteristics of information technology and information technology systems described above.

An unintentionally introduced flaw or defect ("bug") may open the door for opportunistic use of the vulnerability by an adversary who learns of its existence. Many vulnerabilities are widely publicized after they are discovered and can then be used by anyone with moderate technical skills until a patch can be developed, disseminated, and installed. Intruders with the time and resources may also discover unintentional defects that they protect as valuable secrets that can be used when necessary. As long as those defects go unaddressed, the vulnerabilities they create can be used by the intruder.

An intentionally introduced flaw has the same effect as an unintentionally introduced one, except that the adversary does not have to wait to learn of its existence, and the adversary can take advantage of it as soon as it suits his purposes. For example, so-called back doors are sometimes built into programs by their creators; the purpose of a "back door" is to enable another party to bypass security features that would otherwise keep that other party out of the system or network. An illustration would be a back door on the password manager to a system—authorized users would have an assigned login name and password that would enable them to do certain things (and only those things) on the Web site. But if the program's creator had installed a back door, a knowledgeable intruder (perhaps in cahoots with the program's creator) could enter a special

---

[17] See Steve Stasiukonis, "Social Engineering, the USB Way," *Dark Reading*, June 7, 2006, available at http://www.darkreading.com/document.asp?doc_id=95556&WT. svl=column1_1.

40-character password and use any login name and then be able to do anything he wanted on the system.

One particularly problematic vulnerability is known as a "zero-day vulnerability." The term refers to a vulnerability for which the responsible party (e.g., the vendor that provides the software) has not provided a fix, often because the vulnerability is not yet known. Thus, an intruder can often take advantage of a zero-day vulnerability before its becoming publicly known. The zero-day vulnerabilities with the most widespread impact are those in a remotely accessible service that runs by default on all versions of a widely used piece of software—under such circumstances, an intruder could take advantage of the vulnerability in many places nearly simultaneously, with all of the consequences that penetrations of such scale might imply.

Those who discover such vulnerabilities in systems face the question of what to do with them. A private party may choose to report a vulnerability privately to those responsible for maintaining the system so that the vulnerability can be repaired; publicize it widely so that corrective actions can be taken; keep a discovered/known vulnerability for its own purposes; or sell it to the highest bidder. National governments face a similar choice—keep it for future use in some adversarial or offensive cyber operation conducted for national purposes or fix/report it to reduce the susceptibility to penetration of the systems in which that vulnerability is found. National governments as well as nongovernment entities such as organized crime participate in markets to acquire zero-day vulnerabilities for future use.

Last, both cyber exploitations and cyberattacks make use of the same penetration approaches and techniques, and thus may look quite similar to the victim, at least until the nature of the malware involved is ascertained.

3.4.2 Cyber Payloads (Malware)

If an intruder is successful at penetrating a system or network, the intruder must decide what to do next.

A payload is most often a "malware" program that is designed to take hostile action against the system to which it has been delivered. In general, these hostile actions can be anything that could be done by an adversary that has programmed the system. For example, once malware has entered a system, it can be programmed to reproduce and retransmit itself, destroy or alter files on the system, slow the system down, issue bogus commands to equipment attached to the system, monitor traffic going by, copy and send files to a secret e-mail address, create a vulnerability for future use, and so on. The payload is what determines if an adversarial cyber operation is an attack or an exploitation.

Malware can have multiple capabilities when inserted into an adversary system or network—that is, malware can be programmed to do more than one thing. The timing of these actions can also be varied. And if a communications channel to the intruder is available, malware can be remotely updated. Indeed, in some cases, the initially delivered malware consists of nothing more than a mechanism for scanning the penetrated system to determine its technical characteristics and an update mechanism to retrieve the best packages to further the malware's operation.

Malware may be programmed to activate either immediately or when some condition is met. In the second case, the malware sits quietly and does nothing harmful most of the time. However, at the right moment, the program activates itself and proceeds to (for example) destroy or corrupt data, disable system defenses, or introduce false message traffic. The "right moment" can be triggered because:

- A certain date and time are reached;
- The malware receives an explicit instruction to execute;
- The traffic monitored by the malware signals the right moment; or
- Something specific happens in the malware's immediate environment.

Malware may also install itself in ways that keep it from being detected. It may delete itself, leaving behind little or no trace that it was ever present. In some cases, malware can remain even after a computer is scanned with anti-malware software or even when the operating system is reinstalled from scratch.

For example, many computers—including desktop and laptop computers in everyday use—run through a particular power-on sequence when their power is turned on. The computer's power-on sequence loads a small program from a chip inside the computer known as the BIOS (Basic Input-Output System), and then runs the BIOS program. The BIOS program then loads the operating system from another part of the computer, usually its hard drive. Most anti-malware software scans only the operating system on the hard drive, assuming the BIOS chip to be intact. But some malware is designed to modify the program on the BIOS chip, and reinstalling the operating system simply does not touch the (modified) BIOS program. The Chernobyl virus is an example of malware that targets the BIOS,[18] and in 1998 it rendered several hundred thousand

---

[18] The Chernobyl virus is further documented in CERT Coordination Center, "CIH/Chernobyl Virus," CERT® Incident Note IN-99-03, updated April 26, 1999, available at http://www-uxsup.csx.cam.ac.uk/pub/webmirrors/www.cert.org/incident_notes/IN-99-03.html.

computers entirely inoperative without physical replacement of the BIOS chip.

Last, the payload might not take the form of hostile software at all. For example, an intruder might use a particular access path and take advantage of a certain vulnerability to give himself remote access to the target computer such that the intruder has all of the privileges and capabilities that he might have if he were sitting at the keyboard of that computer. He is then in a position to issue to the computer commands of his own choosing, and such commands may well have a harmful effect on the target computer.

3.4.3 Operational Considerations

Sections 3.4.1 and 3.4.2 describe the basic structure of hostile activities in cyberspace. But an intruder must take into account a number of operational considerations if such activities are to be successful:

- *Effects prediction and assessment.* When planning a hostile operation, the expected outcome is a factor in weighing its desirability. When the operation has concluded, the responsible party wants to know if it was successful. But accurate predictions about the outcome of hostile operations and assessing the effects of such operations are complex and difficult challenges. Damage to a computer, for example, is invisible to the naked eye.
- *Target selection.* Which specific computers or networks are to be targeted in a hostile cyber operation? And how would they be identified at a distance? Target identification information can come from a number of sources, including open source collection, automated target selection, and manual exploration of possible targets. A high degree of selectivity in targeting may require large amounts of intelligence information.
- *Fragility.* A victim that discovers a penetration is likely to fix the vulnerability that was taken advantage of by an intruder. Thus, an intruder must consider the possibility that a particular penetration tool will be usable only once or a few times.
- *Rules of engagement.* These rules specify what tools may be used to conduct a hostile cyber operation, what their targets may be, what effects may be sought, and who may conduct such operations under what circumstances. Governments in particular expend considerable effort in specifying these rules for a variety of different purposes (e.g., military purposes, intelligence purposes, law enforcement purposes).
- *The availability of intelligence.* As a general rule, a scarcity of intelligence information regarding possible targets means that any cyber operation launched against them can only be "broad-spectrum" and relatively

indiscriminate or blunt. Substantial amounts of intelligence information about targets (and paths to those targets) are required if an operation is intended as a very precise one directed at a particular system. Often, intelligence is gathered in stages, in which an initial exploitation leads to information that can facilitate further exploitation.

3.5 CHARACTERIZING THREATS TO CYBERSECURITY

Malevolent actors in cyberspace span a very broad spectrum, ranging from lone individuals at one extreme to those associated with major nation-states at the other; all pose cybersecurity threats. Organized crime (e.g., drug cartels or extortion rings) and transnational terrorists (and terrorist organizations, some of them state-sponsored) occupy a region between these two extremes, but they are closer to the nation-state than to the lone intruder.

In addition to those who are motivated by pure curiosity, malevolent actors have a range of motivations. Some are motivated by the desire to penetrate or vandalize for the thrill of it, others by the desire to steal or profit from their actions. And still others are motivated by ideological or nationalistic considerations.

The skills of malevolent actors also span a very broad range. Some have only a rudimentary understanding of the underlying technology and are capable only of using tools that others develop to conduct their own operations but in general are not capable of developing new tools. Those with an intermediate level of skill are capable of developing hacking tools on their own.

Those with the most advanced levels of skills—that is, the high-end threat—can identify weaknesses in target systems and networks and develop tools to take advantage of such knowledge. Moreover, they are often supported by large organizations such as nation-states or organized crime syndicates, and may operate in large teams that provide a broad mix of skills including but by no means limited to those specifically related to computer skills. These organizations provide funding, expertise, and support. When governments are involved, the resources of national intelligence, military, and law enforcement services can be brought to bear. Of significant concern to policy makers is the reality that against the high-end intruder, efforts oriented toward countering the casual adversary or even the common cyber criminal amount to little more than speed bumps.

The availability of such resources widens the possible target set of high-end adversaries. Low- and mid-level adversaries often benefit from nonselective targeting—that is, they do not care which specific computers they victimize. For example, an adversary may conduct an operation that seeks the credit card numbers of a group of individuals. The operation may not be entirely successful because some of these individuals have defenses in place that thwart the operation on their individual machines. But the operation taken as a whole will obtain some credit card numbers, and an adversary that simply wants credit card numbers without regard for who actually owns those numbers will regard this operation as a success.

However, because of the resources available to them, high-end adversaries may also be able to target a specific computer or user that has enormous value ("the crown jewels"). In the former case, an adversary confronted with an adequately defended system simply moves on to another system that is not so well defended. In the latter case, the adversary has the resources to escalate the operation against a specific target to a very high degree—perhaps overwhelmingly so. Box 3.4 describes what has become known as the advanced persistent threat.

High-end adversaries—and especially major nation-state adversaries—are also likely to have the resources that allow them to obtain detailed information about the target system, such as knowledge gained by having access to the source code of the software running on the target or the schematics of the target device, or through reverse-engineering. Success in obtaining such information is not guaranteed, of

---

BOX 3.4 The Advanced Persistent Threat

Discussions of high-end cybersecurity threats often make reference to the "advanced persistent threat (APT)." One document suggests that the term was originally coined by the U.S. Air Force in 2006 to refer to "a sophisticated adversary engaged in [cyber] warfare in support of long-term strategic goals."[1] That is, the APT is a party (an actor) that is technologically advanced and persistent (i.e., able and willing to persist in its efforts).

A second usage of the term refers to the character of a cyber intrusion—one that is technologically sophisticated (i.e., advanced) and hard to find and eliminate (i.e., persistent). In this usage, the APT is highly focused on a particularly valuable target. This tight and narrow focus stands in contrast to other cyber threats (e.g., spamming for credit card numbers) that seek targets of opportunity. An APT typically makes use of tools and techniques that are customized to the specific security configuration and posture of its target. Furthermore, it operates in ways that its perpetrators hope minimize the likelihood of detection.

---

[1] See Fortinet, Inc., "Threats on the Horizon: The Rise of the Advanced Persistent Threat," Solution Brief, 2013, http://www.fortinet.com/sites/default/files/solutionbrief/threats-on-the-horizon-rise-of-advanced-persistent-threats.pdf.

course, but the likelihood of success is clearly an increasing function of the availability of resources. For instance, a country may obtain source code and schematics of a certain vendor's product because it can require that the vendor make those available to its intelligence agencies as a condition of permitting the vendor to sell products within its borders.

The high-end adversary is generally indifferent to the form that its path to success takes, as long as that path meets various constraints such as affordability and secrecy. In particular, the high-end adversary will trick or blackmail a trusted insider to do its bidding or infiltrate a target organization with a trained agent rather than crack a security system if the former is easier to do than the latter.

To support this broad range of malevolent actors, there is a thriving and robust underground marketplace for hacking tools and services. Those wishing to conduct an adversarial operation in cyberspace can often purchase the service with nothing more than a credit card (probably a stolen one) or an alternative and untraceable currency such as Bitcoin.[19] Design and customization of tools is also available, as are piece parts out of which a malevolent actor can assemble his own adversarial cyber operation. In an environment in which such services can be bought and sold, the universe of possible adversaries expands enormously.

A number of general observations can be made about the various malevolent actors:

- Bad guys who want to have an effect on their targets have some motivation to keep trying, even if their initial efforts are not successful in intruding on a victim's computer systems or networks.
- Bad guys nearly always make use of deception in some form— they trick the victim into doing something that is contrary to the victim's interests.
- A would-be bad guy who is induced or persuaded in some way to refrain from intruding on a victim's computer systems or networks results in no harm to those systems or networks, and such an outcome is just as good as thwarting his hostile operation (and may be better if the user is persuaded to avoid conducting such operations in the future).
- Cyber bad guys will be with us forever for the same reason that crime will be with us forever—as long as the information stored in, processed by, or carried through a computer system or network has value to

---

[19] Bitcoin is a digital currency that was launched in 2009. See, for example, François R. Velde, "Bitcoin: A Primer," *Chicago Fed Letter*, Number 517, December 2013, available at http://www.chicagofed.org/digital_assets/publications/chicago_fed_letter/2013/cfldecember2013_317.pdf.

third parties, cyber bad guys will have some reason to conduct adversarial operations against a potential victim's computer systems and networks.

3.6 THREAT ASSESSMENT

The process through which information is assembled and interpreted to assess the threats faced by a potential target is known as threat assessment. Threat assessments help those who are defending systems and networks to allocate resources (money, time, effort, personnel) *prior* to hostile action and to plan what they should do when they are the target of such action. For example, a threat assessment may suggest that more resources should be deployed to combat one particular threat over all others or that a particular strategy would be more effective than others in responding to a given threat.

In general, threat assessments are based on information from multiple sources. As is discussed in Section 4.1.4, successful forensics of actual cyber incidents provide one kind of information, yielding details about the methodology and identity of the intruders, the damage that resulted, and so on. Other sources of useful information may include intercepts of communications and other signals, interviews with those knowledgeable about intruder doctrine or operations, analysis of intruders' documents, photo reconnaissance, reports from intelligence agents, public writing and speeches by relevant parties, and so on.

A threat assessment sheds light on adversary capabilities and intentions. ("Adversary" in this context can refer to more than one potentially hostile party.) What an adversary is capable of doing depends on the tools available, the skill with which the adversary can use those tools, and the numbers of skilled personnel available to the adversary. What an adversary intends to do depends on the adversary's motivation, as described above. Motivation and intent are reflected in the adversary's target set (i.e., what targets the adversary seeks to penetrate) and in what the adversary wishes to do or be able to do once penetration is achieved (e.g., exfiltrate information, destroy data).

4

Enhancing Cybersecurity

4.1 APPROACHES TO IMPROVING SECURITY

There are several approaches to minimizing the number and significance of adversarial cyber operations. The approaches described below are not mutually exclusive, and robust cybersecurity generally requires that some combination of them be used.

4.1.1 Reducing Reliance on Information Technology

The most basic way to improve cybersecurity is to reduce the use of information technology (IT) in critical contexts. Thus, the advantages of using IT must be weighed against the security risks that the use of IT might entail. In some cases, security risks cannot be mitigated to a sufficient degree, and the use of IT should be rejected. In other cases, security risks can be mitigated with some degree of effort and expense—these costs should be factored into the decision. But what should *not* happen is that security risks be ignored entirely—as may sometimes be the case.

An example of reducing reliance on IT is a decision to refrain from connecting a computer system to the Internet, even if not connecting might increase costs or decrease the system's utility. The theory underlying such a decision is that the absence of an Internet connection to such a computer will prevent intruders from gaining access to it and thus that the computer system will be safe. In fact, this theory is not right—the lack of such a connection reduces but does not prevent access, and thus the safety of the computer system cannot be taken for granted forever after. But disconnection does help under many circumstances.

The broader point can be illustrated by supervisory control and data acquisition (SCADA) systems, some of which are connected to the Internet.[1] SCADA systems are used to control many elements of physical infrastructure: electric power, gas and oil pipelines, chemical plants, factories, water and sewage, and so on. Infrastructure operators connect their SCADA systems to the Internet to facilitate communications with them, at least in part because connections and communications hardware that are based on standard Internet protocols are often the least expensive way to provide such communications. But Internet connections also potentially provide access paths to these SCADA systems that intruders can use.

Note that disconnection from the Internet may not be easy to accomplish. Although SCADA systems may be taken off the Internet, connecting these systems to administrative computers that are themselves connected to the Internet (as might be useful for optimizing billing, for example) means that these SCADA systems are in fact connected—indirectly—to the Internet.

4.1.2 Knowing That Security Has Been Penetrated

Detection

From the standpoint of an individual system or network operator, the only thing worse than being penetrated is being penetrated and not knowing about it. Detecting that one has been the target of a hostile cyber operation is also the first step toward taking any kind of specific remedial action.

Detection involves a decision that something (e.g., some file, some action) is harmful (or potentially harmful) or not harmful. Making such decisions is problematic because what counts as harmful or not harmful is for the most part a human decision—and such judgments may not be made correctly. In addition, the number of nonharmful things happening inside a computer or a network is generally quite large compared with the number of harmful things going on. So the detection problem is nearly always one of finding needles in haystacks.

One often-used technique for detecting malware is to check to see if a suspect program has been previously identified as being "bad." Such checks depend on "signatures" that might be associated with the program—the name of the program, the size of the program, the date

---

[1] See http://cyberarms.wordpress.com/2013/03/19/worldwide-map-of-internet-connected-scada-systems/.

when it was created, a hash of the program,[2] and so on. Signatures might also be associated with the path through which a program has arrived at the target—where it came from, for example.

The Einstein program of the Department of Homeland Security (DHS) is an example of a signature-based approach to improving cybersecurity.[3] By law and policy, DHS is the primary agency responsible for protecting U.S. government agencies other than the Department of Defense and the intelligence community. Einstein monitors Internet traffic going in and out of government networks and inspects a variety of traffic data (i.e., the header information in each packet but not the content of a packet itself) and compares that data to known patterns of such data that have previously been associated with malware. If the match is sufficiently close, further action can be taken (e.g., a notification of detection made or traffic dropped).

This signature-based technique for detection has two primary weaknesses. First, it is easy to morph the code without affecting what the program can do so that there are an unlimited number of functionally equivalent versions with different signatures. Second, the technique cannot identify a program as malware if the program has never been seen before.

Another technique for detection monitors the behavior of a program; if the program does "bad things," it is identified as malware. When there are behavioral signatures that help with anomaly detection, this technique can be useful. (A behavioral signature can be specified in terms of designating as suspicious any one of a specific set of actions, or it can be behavior that is significantly different from a user's "normal" behavior.) But it is not a general solution because there is usually no reliable way to distinguish between an authorized user who wishes to do something for a legitimate and benign purpose and an intruder who wishes to do that very same thing for some nefarious purpose. In practice, this technique often results in a significant number of false positives—indications that something nefarious is going on when in fact it is not. A high level of false positives annoys legitimate users, and often results in these users being unable to get their work done.

---

[2] One definition of a "hash function" is an algorithm that turns an arbitrary sequence of bits (1's and 0's) into a fixed-length value known as the hash of that string. With a well-constructed algorithm, hashes of two different bit sequences are very unlikely to have the same hash value.

[3] Department of Homeland Security, National Cyber Security Division, Computer Emergency Readiness Team (US-CERT), *Privacy Impact Assessment [of the] Einstein Program: Collecting, Analyzing, and Sharing Computer Security Information Across the Federal Civilian Government*, September 2004, available at http://www.dhs.gov/xlibrary/assets/privacy/privacy_pia_eisntein.pdf.

Assessment

A hostile action taken against an individual system or network may or may not be part of a larger adversary operation that affects many systems simultaneously, and the scale and the nature of the systems and networks affected in an operation are critical information for decision makers.

Detecting a *coordinated* adversary effort against the background noise of ongoing hostile operations also remains an enormous challenge, given that useful information from multiple sites must be made available on a timely basis. (And as detection capabilities improve, adversaries will take steps to mask such signs of coordinated efforts.)

An assessment addresses many factors, including the scale of the hostile cyber operation (how many entities are being targeted), the nature of the targets (which entities are being targeted), the success of the operation and the extent and nature of damage caused by the operation, the extent and nature of any foreign involvement derived from technical analysis of the operation and/or any available intelligence information not specifically derived from the operation itself, and attribution of the operation to a responsible party (discussed further in Box 4.1). Information on such factors is likely to be quite scarce when the first indications are received of "something bad going on in cyberspace." Assessments are further complicated by the possibility that an initial penetration is simply paving the way for hostile payloads that will be delivered later, or by the possibility that the damage done by an adversarial operation will not be visible for a long time after it has taken place.

The government agencies responsible for threat assessment and warning can, in principle, draw on a wide range of information sources, both inside and outside the government. In addition to hearing from private-sector entities that are being targeted, cognizant government agencies can communicate with security IT vendors, such as Symantec and McAfee, that monitor the Internet for signs of hostile activity. Other public interest groups, such as the OpenNet Initiative and the Information Warfare Monitor, seek to monitor hostile operations launched on the Internet.[4]

---

[4] See the OpenNet Initiative (http://opennet.net/) and the Information Warfare Monitor (http://www.infowar-monitor.net/) Web sites for more information on these groups. A useful press report on the activities of these groups can be found at Kim Hart, "A New Breed of Hackers Tracks Online Acts of War," *Washington Post*, August 27, 2008, available at http://www.washingtonpost.com/wp-dyn/content/article/2008/08/26/AR2008082603128_pf.html.

4.1.3 Defending a System or Network

Defending a system or network means taking actions so that a hostile actor is less successful than he or she would otherwise be in the absence of defensive actions. A desirable side effect of taking such measures is that by reducing the likelihood that a hostile actor will succeed, that actor may also be deterred from taking hostile action because of its possible futility.

Some of the most important approaches to defense include:

- *Reducing the number of vulnerabilities contained in any deployed IT system or network.* There are two methods for doing so.
  - Fix vulnerabilities as soon as they become known (a method known as "patching"). Much software has the capability to update itself, and many updates received automatically by a system contain patches that repair vulnerabilities that have become known since the software was released for general use.
  - Design and implement software so that it has fewer vulnerabilities from the start. Software designers know many principles about how to design and build IT systems and networks more securely (Box 4.2). Systems or networks not built in accord with such principles will almost certainly exhibit inherent vulnerabilities that are difficult or impossible to address. In some cases, hardware-based security features are feasible—implementing such features in hardware is often more secure than implementing them in software, although hardware implementations may be less flexible than comparable software implementations.
- *Eliminating or blocking known but unnecessary access paths.* Many IT systems or networks have a variety of ways to access them that are unnecessary for their effective use. Security-conscious system administrators often disconnect unneeded wireless connections and wired jacks; disable USB ports; change system access controls to quickly remove departing employees or to restrict the access privileges available to individual users to only those that are absolutely necessary for their work; and install firewalls that block traffic from certain suspect sources. Disconnecting from the Internet is a particular instance of eliminating an access path.
- *"Whitelisting" software.* Vendors of major operating systems provide the option of (and sometimes require) restricting the programs that can be run to those whose provenance can be demonstrated. An example of this approach is the "app store" approach to software development by third parties for mobile devices. In principle, whitelisting requires that the code of an application be cryptographically signed by its author using a public digital certification of identity, and thus a responsible party can be identi-

BOX 4.1 On Attribution

Attribution is the process through which an adversarial cyber operation is associated with its perpetrator. In this context, the definition of "perpetrator" can have many meanings:

- The computer from which the adversarial cyber operation reached the target. Note that this computer—the one most proximate to the target—may well belong to an innocent third party that has no knowledge of the operation being conducted.
- The computer that launched or initiated the operation.
- The geographic location of the machine that launched or initiated the operation.
- The individual sitting at the keyboard of the initiating machine.
- The nation under whose jurisdiction the named individual falls (e.g., by virtue of his physical location when he typed the initiating commands).
- The entity under whose auspices the individual acted, if any.

One can thus imagine a hostile operation that is launched under the auspices of Elbonia, by a Ruritanian citizen sitting in a Darkistanian computer laboratory, that penetrates computers in Agraria as intermediate nodes in an attack on computers in Latkovia.

In general, "attribution" of a hostile cyber operation could refer to an identification of any of three entities:

- A computer or computers (called C) that may be involved in the operation. The identity of C may be specified as a machine serial number, a MAC address, or an Internet Protocol (IP) address.[1]
- The human being(s) (H) involved in the operation, especially the human being who initiates the hostile operation (e.g., at the keyboard). The identity of H may be specified as his or her name, pseudonym, or identification card number, for example.
- The party (P) ultimately responsible for the actions of the involved humans. The identity of P may be the name of another individual, the name of an organization, or the name of a country, for example. If H is a "lone wolf," P and H are probably the same.

Note that knowing the identity of C does not necessarily identify H, and knowing the identity of H does not necessarily identify P.

The distinctions between C, H, and P are important because the appropriate meaning of attribution depends on the reason that attribution is necessary.

- If the goal is to mitigate the negative effects of a hostile cyber operation as soon as possible, it is necessary to shut down the computers involved in the operation, a task that depends on affecting the computers more than on affecting their operators or their masters. The identity of C is important.
- If the goal is to prosecute or take the responsible humans into custody, the names of these human beings are important. The identity of H is important.
- If the goal is to deter future hostile acts, and recognizing that deterrence involves imposing a cost on the party that would otherwise choose to launch a future hostile act, the identity of P is important.

When the identities of H or P are desired, judgments of attribution are based on all available sources of information, which could include technical signatures and forensics collected regarding the act in question, communications information (e.g., intercepted phone calls monitoring conversations of individuals or their leaders), prior history (e.g., similarity to previous hostile operations), and knowledge of those with incentives to conduct such operations.

The fact that such a diversity of sources is necessary for identifying humans underscores a fundamental point—assignment of responsibility for an adversarial cyber operation is an act that is influenced although not uniquely determined by the technical information associated with the operation itself. Nontechnical evidence can often play an important role in determining responsibility, and ultimately, human judgment is an essential element of any attempt at attribution.

It is commonly said that attribution of an adversarial cyber operation is impossible. The statement does have an essential kernel of truth: if the perpetrator makes no mistakes, uses techniques that have never been seen before, leaves behind no clues that point to himself, does not discuss the operation in any public or monitored forum, and does not conduct his actions during a period in which his incentives to conduct such operations are known publicly, then identification of the perpetrator may well be impossible.

Indeed, sometimes all of these conditions are met, and policy makers rightly despair of their ability to act appropriately under such circumstances. But in other cases, the problem of attribution is not so dire, because one or more of these conditions are not met, and it may be possible to make some useful (if incomplete) judgments about attribution. For example, a cyber intruder may leave his IP address exposed (perhaps because he forgot to use an anonymizing service to hide it). That IP address may be the key piece of information that is necessary to track the intruder's location and eventually to arrest the individual involved.[2]

Perhaps the more important point is that *prompt* attribution of any given adversarial cyber operation is much more difficult than *eventual* or *delayed* attribution. It takes time—days, weeks, perhaps months—to assemble forensic evidence and to compare it to evidence of previous operations, to query nontechnical intelligence sources, and so on. In a national security context, policy makers faced with responding to a hostile cyber operation naturally feel pressure to respond quickly, but sometimes such pressures have more political than operational significance.

Last, because attribution to any actor beyond a machine involves human judgments, actors that are accused of being responsible for bad actions in cyberspace can always assert their innocence and point to the sinister motives of the parties making human judgments, regardless of whether those judgments are well founded. Such denials have some plausibility, especially in an environment in which there are no accepted standards for making judgments related to attribution.

---

[1] A MAC address (MAC is an acronym for media access control) is a unique number associated with a physical network adapter, specified by the manufacturer and hard-coded into the adapter hardware. An IP address (Internet Protocol address) is a number assigned by the operator of a network using the Internet Protocol to a device (e.g., a computer) attached to that network; the operator may, or may not, use a configuration protocol that assigns a new number every time the device appears on the network.

[2] See Gerry Smith, "FBI Agent: We've Dismantled the Leaders of Anonymous," *The Huffington Post*, August 21, 2013, available at http://www.huffingtonpost.com/2013/08/21/anonymous-arrests-fbi_n_3780980.html.

**BOX 4.2 The Saltzer-Schroeder Principles of
Secure System Design and Development**

Saltzer and Schroeder articulate eight design principles that can guide system design and contribute to an implementation without security flaws:

- *Economy of mechanism: The design should be kept as simple and small as possible.* Design and implementation errors that result in unwanted access paths will not be noticed during normal use (since normal use usually does not include attempts to exercise improper access paths). As a result, techniques such as line-by-line inspection of software and physical examination of hardware that implements protection mechanisms are necessary. For such techniques to be successful, a small and simple design is essential.
- *Fail-safe defaults: Access decisions should be based on permission rather than exclusion.* The default situation is lack of access, and the protection scheme identifies conditions under which access is permitted. The alternative, in which mechanisms attempt to identify conditions under which access should be refused, presents the wrong psychological base for secure system design. This principle applies both to the outward appearance of the protection mechanism and to its underlying implementation.
- *Complete mediation: Every access to every object must be checked for authority.* This principle, when systematically applied, is the primary underpinning of the protection system. It forces a system-wide view of access control, which, in addition to normal operation, includes initialization, recovery, shutdown, and maintenance. It implies that a foolproof method of identifying the source of every request must be devised. It also requires that proposals to gain performance by remembering the result of an authority check be examined skeptically. If a change in authority occurs, such remembered results must be systematically updated.
- *Open design: The design should not be secret.* The protection mechanisms should not depend on the ignorance of potential attackers, but rather on the possession of specific, more easily protected keys or passwords. This decoupling of protection mechanisms from protection keys permits the mechanisms to be examined by many reviewers without concern that the review may itself compromise the safeguards. In addition, any skeptical users may be allowed to convince

fied if the program does damage to the user's system.[5] If the app store does whitelisting consistently and rigorously (and app stores do vary significantly in their rigor), the user is more secure in this arrangement, but cannot run programs that have not been properly signed. Another issue for whitelisting is who establishes any given whitelist—the user (who

---

[5] The whitelisting approach can be extended to other scenarios. For example, a mail service can be configured to accept e-mail only from a specified list of parties approved by the recipient as "safe." A networked computer can be configured to accept connections only from a specified list of computers.

themselves that the system they are about to use is adequate for their individual purposes. Finally, it is simply not realistic to attempt to maintain secrecy for any system that receives wide distribution.

- *Separation of privilege: Where feasible, a protection mechanism that requires two keys to unlock it is more robust and flexible than one that allows access to the presenter of only a single key.* The reason for this greater robustness and flexibility is that, once the mechanism is locked, the two keys can be physically separated, and distinct programs, organizations, or individuals can be made responsible for them. From then on, no single accident, deception, or breach of trust is sufficient to compromise the protected information.

- *Least privilege: Every program and every user of the system should operate using the least set of privileges necessary to complete the job.* This principle reduces the number of potential interactions among privileged programs to the minimum for correct operation, so that unintentional, unwanted, or improper uses of privilege are less likely to occur. Thus, if a question arises related to the possible misuse of a privilege, the number of programs that must be audited is minimized.

- *Least common mechanism: The amount of mechanism common to more than one user and depended on by all users should be minimized.* Every shared mechanism (especially one involving shared variables) represents a potential information path between users and must be designed with great care to ensure that it does not unintentionally compromise security. Further, any mechanism serving all users must be certified to the satisfaction of every user, a job presumably harder than satisfying only one or a few users.

- *Psychological acceptability: It is essential that the human interface be designed for ease of use, so that users routinely and automatically apply the protection mechanisms correctly.* More generally, the use of protection mechanisms should not impose burdens on users that might lead users to avoid or circumvent them—when possible, the use of such mechanisms should confer a benefit that makes users want to use them. Thus, if the protection mechanisms make the system slower or cause the user to do more work—even if that extra work is "easy"—they are arguably flawed.

SOURCE: Adapted from J.H. Saltzer and M.D. Schroeder, "The Protection of Information in Computer Systems," *Proceedings of the IEEE* 63(9):1278-1308, September 1975.

may not have the expertise to determine safe parties) or someone else (who may not be willing or able to provide the full range of applications desired by the user or may accept software too uncritically for inclusion on the whitelist).

These approaches to defense are well known, and are often implemented to a certain degree in many situations. But in general, these approaches have not been adopted as fully as they could be, leaving systems more vulnerable than they would otherwise be. If the approaches remain valid (and they do), why are they not more widely adopted? Several factors account for this phenomenon:

- *Potential conflicts with performance and functionality.* In many cases, closing down access paths and introducing cybersecurity to a system's design slows it down or makes it harder to use. Restricting access privileges to users often has serious usability implications and makes it harder for users to get legitimate work done, as for example when someone needs higher access privileges temporarily but on a time-urgent basis. Implementing the checking, monitoring, and recovery needed for secure operation requires a lot of computation and does not come for free. User demands for backward compatibility at the applications level often call for building into new systems some of the same security vulnerabilities present in the old systems. Program features that enable adversary access can be turned off, but doing so may disable functionality needed or desired by users.
- *The mismatch between these approaches to defense and real-world software development environments.* For example, software developers often experience false starts, and many "first-try" artifacts are thrown away. In such an environment, it makes very little sense to invest up front in the approaches to defense outlined above unless such adherence is relatively inexpensive.
- *The difficulty of upgrading large systems.* With large systems in place, it is very difficult, from both a cost and a deployment standpoint, to upgrade all parts of the system at once. This means that for practical purposes, an organization may well be operating with an information technology environment in which the parts that have not been replaced are likely still vulnerable, and their interconnection to the parts that have been replaced may make even the new components vulnerable.

4.1.4 Ensuring Accountability

Accountability is the ability to unambiguously associate a consequence with a past action of an individual or an organization. Authentication refers to a process that ensures that an asserted identity is indeed properly associated with the asserting party. Access control is the technical mechanism by which certain system privileges but not others are granted to specified individuals. Forensics for cybersecurity are the technical means by which the activity of an intruder can be reconstructed; in many cases, the intruder leaves behind evidence that provides clues to his or her identity.

Individual Authentication and Access Control

For purposes of this report, authentication usually refers to the process of establishing that a particular identifier (such as a login name) correctly refers to a specific party, such as a user, a company, or a government agency.

As applied to individuals, authentication serves two purposes:

• *Ensuring that only authorized parties can perform certain actions.* In many organizations, authorized users are granted a set of privileges—the system is intended to ensure that those users can exercise only those privileges and no others. Because certain users have privileges that others lack, someone who is not authorized to perform a given action may seek to usurp the authentication credentials of someone who is so authorized so that the unauthorized party can impersonate an authorized party. A user may be authorized by virtue of the role(s) he or she plays (e.g., all senior executives have the ability to delete records, but no one else) or by virtue of his or her explicit designation by name (Jane has delete access but John does not).

• *Facilitating accountability,* which is the ability to associate a consequence with a past improper action of an individual. Thus, the authentication process must unambiguously identify one and only one individual who will be held accountable for improper actions. (This is the reason that credentials should not be shared among individuals.) To avoid accountability, an individual may seek to defeat an authentication process.

In general, the authentication process depends on one or more of three factors: something you know, something you have, or something you are.

• *Something you know,* such as a password. Passwords have many advantages. For example, the use of passwords requires no specialized hardware or training. Passwords can be distributed, maintained, and updated by telephone, fax, or e-mail. But they are also susceptible to guessing and to theft.[6] Passwords are easily shared, either intentionally or inadvertently (when written down near a computer, for example), and a complex, expensive infrastructure is necessary to enable resetting lost (forgotten) passwords. Because people often reuse the same name and password combinations across different systems to ease the burden

---

[6] For example, in 2010, the most common passwords for Gawker Media Web sites were (in order of frequency) "123456," "password," and "12345678." See Impact Lab, "The Top 50 Gawker Media Passwords," December 14, 2010, available at http://www.impactlab.net/2010/12/14/the-top-50-gawker-media-passwords/.

on their memories, a successful password attack on a user on one site increases the likelihood that accounts of the same user on other sites can be hacked.

• *Something you have*, such as a cell phone. If a user is locked out of his account because of a forgotten password, a password recovery system can send a text message to the user's cell phone with a special activation code that can be used to reset the password. Although anyone can request a reset link for my user name, only I have access to the specific cell phone on which the activation code is received. Of course, this approach presumes that I have—in advance—told the system my cell phone number at the time of account setup; that is the primary way that the system can associate the specific phone number.

• *Something you are*, such as a fingerprint. Biometric authentication (often called biometrics) is the automatic recognition of human individuals on the basis of behavioral and physiological characteristics. Biometrics have the obvious advantage of authenticating the human, not just the presented token or password. Common biometrics in use today verify fingerprints, retinas, irises, and faces, among other things. The most serious disadvantage of biometric credentials is that they can be forged or stolen,[7] and revocation of biometric credentials is difficult (i.e., a biometric credential cannot be changed). Other downsides to biometrics include the fact that not all people can use all systems, making a backup authentication method necessary (and consequently increasing vulnerability), and the fact that remote enrollment of a biometric measure (sending one's fingerprint or iris scan over the Internet, for example) may defeat the purpose and is easily compromised.

These factors can be combined to provide greater authentication security. For example, biometrics (e.g., a fingerprint) or a personal identification number can be used to authenticate a smart identification card that is read by a computer. This approach would provide two-factor authentication—authentication that requires confirmation of two factors rather than one to enable access.

All authentication mechanisms are susceptible to compromise to varying degrees in two ways. One is technical—use of a gummy bear to fake a fingerprint (see Footnote 7) or use of a password-guessing program are examples. The other is social (or psychological)—someone with the

---

[7] For example, in 2002, a security expert was able to fool a number of fingerprint sensors by lifting latent fingerprints from a water glass using soft gummy bear candy. See John Leyden, "Gummi Bears Defeat Fingerprint Sensors: Sticky Problem for Biometrics Firms," *The Register*, May 16, 2002, http://www.theregister.co.uk/2002/05/16/gummi_bears_defeat_fingerprint_sensors/.

necessary privileges can be bribed, tricked, coerced, or extorted into taking action on behalf of someone without those privileges.

Organizational Authentication

At the organizational level, authentication is commonly used to ensure that communications with an organization are in fact being held with the proper organization. For example, if I use the online services of the XYZZY National Bank, I need to be sure that the Web site called www.xyzzynationalbank.com is indeed operated by the XYZZY National Bank. On the Internet today, I would likely rely on the assurances of a trusted third party known as a certificate authority (CA). Certificate authorities (Box 4.3) verify identity based on information that only the proper party

---

BOX 4.3 Certificate Authorities

Cryptography refers to a set of techniques that can be used to scramble information so that only certain parties—parties with the decryption key—can recover the original information. To scramble the original information, the sender of the information uses an encryption key.

In symmetric cryptography (or equivalently, secret-key cryptography), the encryption key is the same as the decryption key; thus, message privacy depends on the key being kept secret. In asymmetric (or, equivalently, public-key) cryptographic systems, the encryption key is different from the decryption key. Message privacy depends only on the decryption key being kept secret. The encryption key can even be published and disseminated widely, so that anyone can encrypt messages.

Certificate authorities are used to facilitate public-key cryptography systems that enable secure communications among a large number of parties who do not know each other and who have not made prior arrangements for communicating. For Alice to send a secure message to Bob, Alice needs to know Bob's encryption key. Alice looks up in a published directory Bob's encryption key (which happens to be 2375959), and then sends an encrypted message to Bob. Only Bob can decrypt it, because only Bob knows the correct decryption key. But how is Alice to know that the number 2375959 does in fact belong to Bob—in other words, how does Alice know that the published directory is trustworthy?

The answer is that a trusted certificate authority stands behind the association between a given encryption key and the party to which it belongs. Certificate authorities play the role of trusted third parties—trusted by both sender and receiver to associate and publish public keys and names of potential message recipients.

Certificate authorities can exist within a single organization, across multiple related organizations, or across society in general. Any number of certificate authorities can coexist, and they may or may not have agreements for cross-certification, whereby if one authority certifies a given person, then another authority will accept that certification within its own structure.

would know, and they issue computer-readable certificates to, for example, the XYZZY National Bank. Users (through their Internet browsers) can automatically check these certificates when they communicate with a Web site operated by a party claiming to be the XYZZY Bank.

Given the role of the CA, its compromise is a dangerous event that can undermine transactions based on assurances of identity. Indeed, certificate authorities have in the past been tricked into issuing bad certificates, and some have even gone rogue on their own. The security of the Internet is under stress today in part because the number of trusted but not trustworthy CAs is growing. Thus, CAs must do what they can to ensure that the certificates for which they are responsible are not compromised and, just as important, must be able to revoke a certificate if and when it is compromised.

Of course, certificate revocation is only half the battle when a certificate is compromised—users relying on a certificate should, in principle, check its status to see if it *has* been revoked. Few users are so diligent— they rely on software to perform such checks. Sometimes the software fails to perform a check, leaving the user with a false sense of security. And sometimes the software informs the user that the certificate has been revoked and asks the user if he or she wants to proceed. Faced with this question, the user often proceeds.

Furthermore, there is an inherent tension between authentication and privacy, because the act of authentication involves some disclosure and confirmation of personal information. Establishing an identifier or attribute for use within an authentication system, creating transactional records, and revealing information used in authentication to others with unrelated interests all have implications for privacy and other civil liberties.

Stronger Authentication for the Internet

As discussed in Chapter 2, digital information is inherently anonymous, which means that specific mechanisms must be in place to associate a given party with any given piece of information. The Internet is a means for transporting information from one computer to another, but today's Internet protocols do not require a validated identity to be associated with the packets that are sent.

Nevertheless, nearly all users of the Internet obtain service through an Internet service provider, and the ISP usually does have—for billing purposes—information about the party sending or receiving any given packet. In other words, access to the Internet usually requires some kind of authentication of identity, but the architecture of the Internet does not require that identity to be carried with sent packets all the way to the intended recipient. (As an important aside, an ISP knows only who pays a bill for Internet service, and one bill may well cover Internet access for multiple users. However, the paying entity may itself have accounting systems in place to differentiate among these multiple users.)

In the name of greater security, proposals have been made for a "strongly authenticated" Internet as a solution to the problem of attribution. Recall that attribution refers to the identification of the entity responsible for a cyber incident. If cyber incidents effectuated through the Internet could be associated with an identifiable entity, accountability could be established and penalties meted out for illegal, improper, or unauthorized actions. "Strong" authentication mechanisms are one way to improve attribution capabilities.

Strong authentication could be one of the more centralized security services provided at the packet level of the Internet, as described in Chapter 2. Alternatively, strong authentication could be a service implemented at the applications level, in which case authentication would be the responsibility of individual applications developers that would then design such services as needed for the particular application in question.

Although the availability of a strongly authenticated Internet would certainly improve the security environment over that of today, it is not a panacea. Perhaps most important, users of a strongly authenticated Internet would be high-priority targets themselves. Once they were compromised (likely through social engineering), their credentials could then be used to gain access to the resources on the strongly authenticated Internet. The intruder could then use these resources to launch further hostile operations against the true target, masking his true identity.

In addition, strong authentication, especially if implemented at the packet level, raises a number of civil liberties concerns, as described in Chapter 5.

Forensics

In a cybersecurity context, the term "cyber forensics" refers to the art and science of obtaining useful evidence from an ostensibly hostile cyber event. Cyber forensics are intended to provide information about what an intruder did and how he or she did it, and to the extent possible to associate a specific party with that event—that is, to attribute the event. Cyber forensics are necessary because, among other things, intruders often seek to cover their tracks.

When digital information is involved, forensics can be difficult. Digital information carries with it no physical signature that can be associated unambiguously with an individual. For example, although a digital signature on a document says something about the computer that signed the

document using a private and secret cryptographic key, it does not necessarily follow that the individual associated with that key signed the document. Because the key is a long string of digits, it is almost certainly stored
in machine-readable form, and the association of the individual with the
signed document requires a demonstration that no one else could have
gained access to that key. Another example is the assumption—often not
true in practice—that the owner of a Wi-Fi router has willfully allowed
all traffic that is carried through it.

Typical forensic tasks include the examination of computer hardware
for information that the perpetrator of a hostile action may have tried to
delete or did not know was recorded, audits of system logs for reconstruc-
tions of a perpetrator's system accesses and activities, statistical and historical analyses of message traffic, and interviews with system users. For
example, system logs may record the fact that someone has downloaded
a very large number of files in a very short time. Such behavior is often
suspicious, and an audit of system logs should flag such behavior for
further review and investigation. Conducted in real time, an audit could
send a warning to system administrators of wrongdoing in progress.

Precisely what must be done in any cyber forensic investigation
depends on its purpose. One purpose, of course, is to obtain evidence
that may be usable in court for a criminal prosecution of the perpetrator.
In this event, forensic investigation also involves maintaining a chain of
custody over the evidence at every step, an aspect of the investigation
that is likely to slow down the investigation. But businesses may need
to conduct a forensic investigation to detect employee wrongdoing or to
protect intellectual property. For this purpose, the evidentiary requirements of forensic investigation may be less stringent and the investigation
shorter, a fact that might allow statistical likelihood, indirect evidence,
and hearsay to fall within the scope of non-evidentiary forensics; the
same may be true in a national security context as well. Business forensic
approaches range across a broad spectrum from traffic analysis tools and
instrumentation of embedded systems to handling massive data volume
and network monitoring, and they require a similar foundation to deal
with increasing complexity and broader application. These points are also
relevant to civil proceedings, both because the standards of proof there are
lower and because the use of digital forensics in business activities may
also be the subject of litigation.

Also, the forensic investigator must proceed differently in an after-
the-fact investigation than in a real-time investigation. Law enforcement
authorities are often oriented toward after-the-fact forensics, which help
to assemble evidence needed for prosecution. But to the extent that pre-
vention or mitigation of damage is the goal of law enforcement authorities

or business operators, real-time or near-real-time forensics may be more valuable.

When cyber forensics are performed on IT systems and networks within the victim's legitimate span of control, the legal and policy issues are few. Such issues become much more complicated if it is necessary to perform cyber forensics on IT systems and networks outside the victim's legitimate span of control. For example, if an adversary has conducted a hostile operation from the computer belonging to an innocent third party that has no relationship to either adversary or victim, conducting forensics on that computer without the third party's knowledge or permission raises a number of legal and policy problems.

4.1.5 Building a Capacity for Containment, Recovery, and Resilience

Acknowledging that defenses are likely to be breached, one can also seek to contain the damage that a breach might cause and/or to recover from the damage that was caused.

Containment

Containment refers to the process of limiting the effects of a hostile action once it occurs. An example is sandboxing. A sandbox is a computing environment designed to be disposable—corruption or compromise in this environment does not matter much to the user, and the intruder is unlikely to gain much in the way of additional resources or privileges. The sandbox can thus be seen as a buffer between the outside world and the "real" computing environment in which serious business can be undertaken. The technical challenge in sandboxing is to develop methods for safe interaction between the buffer and the "real" environment, and in an imperfectly designed disposable environment, unsafe actions can have an effect outside the sandbox. Nevertheless, a number of practical sandboxing systems have been deployed for regular use; these systems provide some level of protection against the dangers of running untrusted programs.

A second example of containment is the use of heterogeneous computing environments. In agriculture, monocultures are known to be highly vulnerable to blight. In a computer security context, a population of millions of identically programmed computers is systematically vulnerable to an exploit that targets a specific security defect, especially if all of those computers are attached to the Internet—a hostile operation that is successful against one of these computers will be successful against all of them, and malware can propagate rapidly in such an environment. If these computers are programmed differently (while still providing the same functionality to the user), the techniques used in a hostile operation against a particular programming base may well be unsuccessful against a different code base, and thus not all of the computers in the population will be vulnerable to those techniques. However, it is generally more expensive and labor-intensive to support a heterogeneous computing environment, and interoperability among the systems in the population may be more difficult to achieve.

Recovery

In general, recovery-oriented approaches accomplish repair by restoring a system to its state at an earlier point in time. If that point in time is too recent, then the restoration will include the damage to the system caused by the attack. If that point in time is too far back, an unacceptable amount of useful work may be lost. A good example is restoring a backup of a computer's files; the first question that the user asks when a backup file is needed is, When was my most recent backup?

A recovery-oriented approach is not particularly useful in any environment in which the attack causes effects on physical systems—if an attack causes a generator to explode, no amount of recovery on the computer systems attacked will restore that generator to working order. (But the operator still needs to restore the computer so that the replacement generator won't be similarly damaged.)

In large systems or services, reverting to a known system state before the security breach may well be infeasible. Under such circumstances, a more practical goal is to restore normal system capacity/functionality with as little loss of operating data as possible.

Resilience

A resilient system is one whose performance degrades gradually rather than catastrophically when its other defensive mechanisms are insufficient to stem an attack. A resilient system will still continue to perform some of its intended functions, although perhaps more slowly or for fewer people or with fewer applications.

Redundancy is one way to provide a measure of resilience. For example, Internet protocols for transmitting information are designed to account for the loss of intermediate nodes—that is, to provide redundant paths in most cases for information to flow between two points.

A second approach to achieving resilience is to design a system or network without a single point of failure—that is, it should be impossible to cause the system or network to cease functioning entirely by crippling or disabling any one component of the system. Unfortunately, discovering single points of failure is sometimes difficult because the system or network in question is so complex. Moreover, the easiest way to achieve redundancy for certain systems is simply to replicate the system and run the different replications together. But if one version has a flaw, simple replication of that version replicates the flaw as well.

4.1.6 Employing Active Defense

The limitations of the measures described above to protect important information technology assets and the information they contain are well known. Many measures (e.g., repair of system vulnerabilities) can be applied only to IT assets within an organization's span of control—that is, systems and networks that it has the legal right to access, monitor, and modify. These also may reduce important functionality in the systems being protected—they become more difficult, slower, and inconvenient to use. They are also reactive—they are invoked or become operational only when a hostile operation has been recognized as having occurred (or is occurring).

Recognizing the limitations of passive defense measures as the only option for responding to the cyber threat, the Department of Defense issued in 2011 its *Department of Defense Strategy for Operating in Cyberspace*, which states that the United States will employ "an active cyber defense capability to prevent intrusions onto DoD networks and systems," defining active cyber defense as "DoD's synchronized, real-time capability to discover, detect, analyze, and mitigate threats and vulnerabilities."[8]

The DOD does not describe active cyber defense in any detail, but the formulation above for "active cyber defense" could, if read broadly, include any action outside the DOD's organizational span of control, any non-cooperative measure affecting or harming an attacker's IT systems and networks, any proactive measure, or any retaliatory measure, as long as such action was taken for the purpose of defending DOD systems or networks from that attacker.

The sections below describe some of the components that a strategy of active cyber defense might logically entail.

Cyber Deception for Defensive Purposes

Deception is often a useful defensive technique. For example, an intruder bent on cyber exploitation seeks useful information. An intruder that can be fooled into exfiltrating false or misleading information that

---

[8] See U.S. Department of Defense, *Department of Defense Strategy for Operating in Cyberspace*, July 2011, available at http://www.defense.gov/news/d20110714cyber.pdf.

looks like the real thing may be misled into taking action harmful to his own interests, and at the very least has been forced to waste time, effort, and resources in obtaining useless information.

The term "honeypot" in computer security jargon refers to a machine, a virtual machine, or other network resource that is intended to act as a decoy or diversion for would-be intruders. Honeypots intentionally contain no real or valuable data and are kept separate from an organization's production systems. Indeed, in most cases, systems administrators *want* intruders to succeed in compromising or breaching the security of honeypots to a certain extent so that they can log all the activity and learn from the techniques and methods used by the intruder. This process allows administrators to be better prepared for hostile operations against their real production systems. Honeypots are very useful for gathering information about new types of operation, new techniques, and information on how things like worms or malicious code propagate through systems, and they are used as much by security researchers as by network security administrators.

When the effects of a honeypot are limited in scope to the victim's systems and networks, the legal and policy issues are relatively limited. But if they have effects on the intruder's systems, both the legal and the policy issues become much more complex. For example, a honeypot belonging to A might contain files of falsified information that themselves carry malware. When the intruder B exfiltrates these files and then views them on B's own systems, the malware in these files is launched and conducts its own offensive operations on B's systems in certain ways.

What might A's malware do on B's systems? It might activate a "beacon" that sends an e-mail to A to report on the environment in which it finds itself, an e-mail that contains enough information to identify B. It might erase files on B's systems. It might install a way for A to penetrate B's systems in the future. All of these actions raise legal and policy issues regarding their propriety.

Disruption

Disruption is intended to reduce the damage being caused by an adversarial cyber operation in progress, usually by affecting the operation of the computer systems being used to conduct the operation.

An example of disrupting an operation in progress would be disabling the computers that control a botnet. Of course, this approach presumes that the controlling computers are known. The first time the botnet is used, such knowledge is unlikely. But over time, patterns of behavior might suggest the identity of those computers and an access path to them. Thus, disruption would be easier to accomplish after repeated attacks.

Under most circumstances, disabling the computers controlling an adversarial operation runs a risk of violating domestic U.S. law such as the Computer Fraud and Abuse Act. However, armed with court orders, information technology vendors and law enforcement authorities have worked together in a number of instances to disrupt the operation of botnets by targeting and seizing servers and controllers associated with those botnets.

An example of such action was a joint Microsoft-Federal Bureau of Investigation effort to take down the Citadel botnet in the May-June 2013 time frame. The effort involved Microsoft filing a civil lawsuit against the Citadel botnet operators. With a court-ordered seizure request and working with U.S. Marshals, employees from Microsoft seized servers from two hosting facilities in New Jersey and Philadelphia.[9] In addition, they provided information about the botnets to computer emergency response teams (CERTs) located abroad, requesting that they target related command-and-control infrastructure. At the same time, the FBI provided related information to its overseas law enforcement counterparts.

Preemption

Preemption—sometimes also known as anticipatory self-defense—is the first use of cyber force against an adversary that is itself about to conduct a hostile cyber action against a victim. The idea of preemption as a part of active defense has been discussed mostly in the context of national security.[10]

Preemption as a defensive strategy is a controversial subject, and the requirements of executing a preemptive strike in cyberspace are substantial.[11] Preemption by definition requires information that an adversary is about to launch a hostile operation that is sufficiently serious to warrant preemption. When the number of possible cyber adversaries is almost limitless, how would a country know who was about to launch such an operation? Keeping all such parties under surveillance using cyber means and other intelligence sources would seem to be a quite daunting task

---

[9] Matthew J. Schwartz, "Microsoft, FBI Trumpet Citadel Botnet Takedowns," June 6, 2013, available at http://www.informationweek.com/attacks/microsoft-fbi-trumpet-citadel-botnet-takedowns/d/d-id/1110261?.

[10] Mike McConnell, "How to Win the Cyber War We're Losing," *Washington Post*, February 28, 2010, available at http://www.washingtonpost.com/wp-dyn/content/article/2010/02/25/AR2010022502493.html.

[11] Herbert Lin, "A Virtual Necessity: Some Modest Steps Toward Greater Cybersecurity," *Bulletin of the Atomic Scientists*, September 1, 2012, available at http://www.thebulletin.org/2012/september/virtual-necessity-some-modest-steps-toward-greater-cybersecurity.

and yet necessary in an environment in which threats can originate from nearly anywhere.

Also, an imminent action by an adversary by definition requires that the adversary take nearly all of the measures and make all of the preparations needed to carry out that action. The potential victim considering preemption must thus be able to target the adversary's cyber assets that would be used to launch a hostile operation. But the assets needed to launch a cyberattack are generally inexpensive and/or easily concealed (or made entirely invisible)—reducing the likelihood that a serious damage-limiting preemption could be conducted.

BOX 4.4 A Brief Case Study—
Securing the Internet Against Routing Attacks

The task of securing the routing protocols of the Internet makes a good case study of the nontechnical complexities that can emerge in what might have been thought of as a purely technical problem.

As noted in Chapter 2, the Internet is a network of networks. Each network acts as an autonomous system under a common administration and with common routing policies. BGP is the Internet protocol used to characterize every network to each other, and in particular to every network operated by an Internet service provider (ISP).

In general, the characterization is provided by the ISP responsible for the network, and in part the characterization specifies how that ISP would route traffic to a given destination. A problem arises if and when a malicious ISP in some part of the Internet falsely asserts that it is the right path to a given destination (i.e., it asserts that it would forward traffic to a destination but in fact would not). Traffic sent to that destination can be discarded, causing that destination to appear to be off the net. Further, the malicious ISP might be able to mimic the expected behavior of the correct destination, fooling unsuspecting users into thinking that their traffic has been delivered properly and thus causing further damage.

The technical proposal to mitigate this problem was to have the owner of each region of Internet addresses digitally sign an assertion to the effect that it is the rightful owner (which would be done using cryptographic mechanisms), and then delegate this assertion to the ISP that actually provides access to the addresses, which in turn would validate it by a further signature, and so on as the assertion crossed the Internet. A suspicious ISP trying to decide if a routing assertion is valid could check this series of signed assertions to validate it.

This scheme has a bit of overhead, which is one objection, but it also has another problem—how can a suspicious ISP know that the signed assertion is valid?

4.2 NONTECHNOLOGICAL DIMENSIONS OF CYBERSECURITY

An important lesson that is often lost amidst discussions of cyber-security is that cybersecurity is not only about technology to make us more secure in cyberspace. Indeed, technology is only one aspect of such security, and is arguably not even the most important aspect of security. Box 4.4 provides a brief case study that illustrates this point. The present section discusses a number of the most important nontechnological factors that affect cybersecurity.

It has been signed using some cryptographic key, but the suspicious ISP must know who owns that key. To this end, it is necessary to have a global key distribution and validation scheme, which is called a public-key infrastructure, or PKI. The original proposal was that there would be a "root of trust," an actor that everyone trusted, who would sign a set of assertions about the identities of lower-level entities, and so on until there was a chain of correctness-confirming assertions that linked the assertions of each owner of an address block back to this root of trust.

This idea proved unacceptable for the reason, perhaps obvious to nontechnical people, that there is no actor that everyone—every nation, every corporation, and so on—is willing to trust. If there were such an actor, and if it were to suddenly refuse to validate the identity of some lower-level actor, that lower-level actor would be essentially removed from the Internet. The alternative approach was to have many roots of trust—perhaps each country would be the root of trust for actors within its borders. But this approach, too, is hard to make work in practice—for example, what if a malicious country signs some assertion that an ISP within its border is the best means to reach some range of addresses? How can someone know that this particular root of trust did not in fact have the authority to make assertions about this part of the address space? Somehow one must cross-link the various roots of trust, and the resulting complexity may be too hard to manage.

Schemes that have been proposed to secure the global routing mechanisms of the Internet differ with respect to the overhead, the range of threats to which they are resistant, and so on. But the major problem that all these schemes come up against is the nontechnical problem of building a scheme that can successfully stabilize a global system built out of regions that simply do not trust each other. And of course routing is only part of making a secure and resilient Internet. An ISP that is malicious can make correct routing assertions and then just drop or otherwise disrupt the packets as they are forwarded. The resolution of these sorts of dilemmas seems to depend on an understanding of how to manage trust, not on technical mechanisms for signing identity assertions.

4.2.1 Economics[12]

Many problems of cybersecurity can be understood better from an economic perspective: network externalities, asymmetric information, moral hazard, adverse selection, liability dumping, risk dumping, regulatory frameworks, and tragedy of the commons. Taken together, economic factors go a long way toward explaining why, beyond any technical solutions, cybersecurity is and will be a hard problem to address.

Many actors make decisions that affect cybersecurity: technology vendors, technology service providers, consumers, firms, law enforcement, the intelligence community, and governments (both as technology users and as guardians of the larger social good). Each of these actors gets plenty of blame for being the "problem": if technology vendors would just properly engineer their products, if end users would just use the technology available to them and learn and practice safe behavior, if companies would just invest more in cybersecurity or take it more seriously, if law enforcement would just pursue the bad guys more aggressively, if policy makers would just do a better job of regulation or legislation, and so on.

There is some truth to such assertions, and yet it is important to understand the incentives for these actors to behave as they do. For example, technology vendors have significant financial incentives to gain a first-mover or a first-to-market advantage. But the logic of reducing time to market runs counter to enhancing security, which adds complexity, time, and cost in design and testing while being hard to value or even assess by customers.

In the end-user space, organizational decision makers and individuals do sometimes (perhaps even often) take cybersecurity into account. But these parties have strong incentives to take only those cybersecurity measures that are valuable for addressing their own cybersecurity needs, and few incentives to take measures that primarily benefit the nation as a whole. In other words, cybersecurity is to a large extent a public good; much of the payoff from security investments may be captured by society rather than directly by any individual firm that invests.

For example, an attacker A who wishes to attack victim V will compromise intermediary M's computer facilities in order to attack V. This convoluted routing is done so that V will have a harder time tracing the

---

[12] For an overview of the economic issues underlying cybersecurity, see Tyler Moore, "Introducing the Economics of Cybersecurity: Principles and Policy Options," in National Research Council, *Proceedings of a Workshop on Deterring Cyberattacks: Informing Strategies and Developing Options for U.S. Policy*, pp. 3-24, The National Academies Press, Washington D.C., 2010. An older but still very useful paper is Ross Anderson, "Why Information Security Is Hard—An Economic Perspective," *Proceedings of the 17th Annual Computer Security Applications Conference*, IEEE Computer Society, New Orleans, La., 2001, pp. 358-365.

attack back to A. However, the compromise on M's computers will usually not damage them very much, and indeed M may not even notice that its computers have been compromised. Investments made by M to protect its computers will not benefit M, but will, rather, protect V. But an Internet-using society would clearly benefit if all of the potential intermediaries in the society made such investments. Many similar examples also have economic roots.

Is the national cybersecurity posture resulting from the investment decisions of many individual firms acting in their own self-interest adequate from a societal perspective? To date, the government's assessment of this question yields "no" for an answer—whereas many in the private sector say "yes." This disagreement is at the heart of many disputes about what the nation can and should do about cybersecurity policy.

4.2.2 Psychology

A wide variety of psychological factors and issues are relevant to cybersecurity.

Social Engineering

One definition of "social engineering" is "the art of gaining access to buildings, systems or data by exploiting human psychology, rather than by breaking in or using technical hacking techniques."[13] For example, instead of trying to find a technical way to access a computer, a social engineer might try to trick an employee into divulging his password by posing as an IT support person.

Social engineering is possible because the human beings who install, configure, operate, and use IT systems of interest can be compromised through deception and trickery. Spies working for an intruder may be unknowingly hired by the victim, and more importantly and commonly, users can be deceived into actions that compromise security. No malware operates by informing a human user that "running this program or opening this file will cause your hard disk to be erased"—rather, it tricks the human into running a program with that effect.

Many instances involving the compromise of users or operators involve e-mails, instant messages, and files that are sent to the target at the initiative of the intruder (often posing as someone known to the victim), or other sources that are visited at the initiative of the target. Examples

---

[13] Joan Goodchild, "Social Engineering: The Basics," December 20, 2012, available at http://www.csoonline.com/article/514063/social-engineering-the-basics.

of the latter include links to appealing Web pages and or downloadable software applications, such as those for sharing pictures or music files.

Another channel for social engineering is the service providers on which many organizations and individuals rely. Both individuals and organizations obtain Internet connectivity from Internet service providers. Many organizations make use of external firms to arrange employee travel or to manage their IT security or repair needs. Many organizations also obtain cybersecurity services from third parties, such as a security software vendor that might be bribed or otherwise persuaded to ignore a particular virus. Service providers are potential security vulnerabilities, and thus might well be intermediate targets in an offensive operation directed at the true (ultimate) target.

Decision Making Under Uncertainty

Decision making under conditions of high uncertainty will almost surely characterize U.S. policy makers responding to the first reports of a significant cyber incident, as described above in Section 4.1.2. Under conditions of high uncertainty, crisis decision-making processes are often flawed. Stein describes a number of issues that affect decision making in this context.[14]

For example, under the category of factors affecting a rational decision-making process, Stein points to uncertainty about realities on the ground as an important influence. In this view, decision making yields suboptimal outcomes because the actors involved do not have or understand all of the relevant information about the situation. Uncertainties may relate to the actual balance of power (e.g., difficulties of cyber threat assessment), the intentions of the various actors (e.g., defensive actions by A are seen as provocative by B, inadvertent actions by A are seen as deliberate by B), the bureaucratic interests pushing decision makers in certain directions (e.g., cyber warriors pushing for operational use of cyber tools), and the significance of an actor's violation of generally accepted norms.

Under the category of psychological factors influencing decision making, Stein points out that because the information-processing capability of people is limited, they are forced in confusing situations to use a variety of cognitive shortcuts and heuristics to "simplify complexity, manage uncertainty, handle information, make inferences, and generate threat perceptions."[15] For example, people often:

---

[14] Janice Gross Stein, "Threat Perception in International Relations," in *The Oxford Handbook of Political Psychology*, 2nd Edition, Leonie Huddy, David O. Sears, and Jack S. Levy (eds.), Oxford University Press, 2013.

[15] Stein, "Threat Perception in International Relations," 2013.

- Interpret ambiguous information in terms of what is most easily available in their cognitive repertoire (availability). Thus, if a cyber disaster (real or hypothetical) is easily recalled, ambiguous information about cyber events will seem to point to a cyber disaster.
- Exaggerate similarities between one event and a prior class of events, typically leading to significant errors in probability judgments or estimates of frequency (representativeness). Thus, if the available information on a cyber event seems to point to its being a hostile action taken by a nation-state, it will be interpreted that way even if that nation-state has taken few such actions in the past.
- Estimate magnitude or degree by comparing it with an "available" initial value (often an inaccurate one) as a reference point and making a comparison (anchoring).
- Attribute the behavior of adversaries in terms of their disposition and animus but attribute their own behavior to situational factors. That is, "they" take certain actions because they want to challenge us, but "we" take the same actions because circumstances demanded that we do so.

Education for Security Awareness and Behavior

Users are a key component of any information technology system in use, and inappropriate or unsafe user behavior on such a system can easily lead to reduced security. Security education has two essential components: security awareness and security-responsible behavior.

- Security awareness refers to user consciousness of the reality and significance of threats and risks to information resources, and it is what motivates users to adopt safeguards that reduce the likelihood of security compromises and/or the effect of such compromises when they do occur.
- Security-responsible behavior refers to what users should and should not do from a security standpoint once they are motivated to take action.

To promote security awareness, various reports have sought to make the public aware of the importance of cybersecurity. In general, these reports point to the sophistication of the cybersecurity threat, the scale of the costs to society as a whole resulting from threats to cybersecurity, and the urgency of "doing something" about the threat. But it is also likely that such reports do not motivate individual users to take cybersecurity more seriously than would a specific targeted and demonstrated threat that could entail substantial personal costs to them.

As for security-responsible behavior, most children do receive some education when it comes to physical security. For example, they are taught to use locks on doors, to recognize dangerous situations, to seek help when confronted with suspicious situations, and so on. But a comparable effort to educate children about some of the basic elements of cybersecurity does not appear to exist.

To illustrate some of what might be included in education for security-responsible behavior, a course taught at the University of Washington in 2006, intended to provide a broad education in the fundamentals of information technology for lay people, set forth the following objectives for its unit on cybersecurity:[16]

- Learn to create strong passwords.
- Set up junk e-mail filtering.
- Use Windows Update to keep your system up to date.
- Update McAfee VirusScan so that you can detect viruses.
- Use Windows Defender to locate and remove spyware.

Convenience and Ease of Use

Security features are often too complex for organizations or individuals to manage effectively or to use conveniently. Security is hard for users, administrators, and developers to understand, making it all too easy to use, configure, or operate systems in ways that are inadvertently insecure. Moreover, security and privacy technologies originally were developed in a context in which system administrators had primary responsibility for security and privacy protections and in which the users tended to be sophisticated. Today, the user base is much wider—including the vast majority of employees in many organizations and a large fraction of households—but the basic models for security and privacy are essentially unchanged.

Security features can be clumsy and awkward to use and can present significant obstacles to getting work done. As a result, cybersecurity measures are all too often disabled or bypassed by the users they are intended to protect. Because the intent of security is to make a system completely unusable to an unauthorized party but completely usable to an authorized one, desires for security and desires for convenience or ease of access are often in tension—and usable security seeks to find a proper balance between the two.

For example, users often want to transfer data electronically between two systems because it is much easier than rekeying the data by hand.

---

[16] See University of Washington, "Lab 11—Computer Security Basics," Winter 2006, available at http://www.cs.washington.edu/education/courses/100/06wi/labs/lab11/lab11.html.

But establishing an electronic link between the systems may add an access path that is useful to an intruder. Taking into account the needs of usable security might call for establishing the link but protecting it or tearing down the link after the data has been transferred.

In other cases, security techniques do not transfer well from one technology to another. For example, it is much more difficult to type a long password on a mobile device than on a keyboard, and yet many mobile applications for a Web service require users to use the same password for access as they do for the desktop computer equivalent.

Also, usable security has social and organizational dimensions as well as technological and psychological ones. Researchers have found that the development of usable security requires deep insight into the human-interaction dimensions of the application for which security is being developed and of the alignment of technical protocols for security and of the social/organizational protocols that surround such security.

4.2.3 Law

U.S. domestic law, international law, and foreign domestic law affect cybersecurity in a number of ways.

Domestic Law

The Congressional Research Service has identified more than 50 federal statutes addressing various aspects of cybersecurity either directly or indirectly.[17] (The acts discussed below are listed with the date of original passage, and "as amended" should be understood with each act.)

Several statutes protect computers and data by criminalizing certain actions. These statutes include the Computer Fraud and Abuse Act of 1986 (prohibits various intrusions on federal computer systems or on computer systems used by banks or in interstate and foreign commerce); the Electronic Communications Privacy Act of 1986 (ECPA; prohibits unauthorized electronic eavesdropping); the Economic Espionage Act of 1996 (outlaws theft of trade secret information, including electronically stored information, if "reasonable measures" have been taken to keep it secret); the Federal Wiretap Act of 1968 as amended (often known as Title III; prohibits real-time surveillance of electronic communications by unauthorized parties); and the Foreign Intelligence Surveillance Act of 1978 (FISA; establishes a framework for the use of "electronic surveil-

---

[17] Eric A. Fischer, *Federal Laws Relating to Cybersecurity: Overview and Discussion of Proposed Revisions*, Congressional Research Service, R42114, June 20, 2013, available at http://www.fas.org/sgp/crs/natsec/R42114.pdf.

lance" conducted to obtain information about a foreign power or foreign territory that relates to the national defense, the security, or the conduct of the foreign affairs of the United States, also known as "foreign intelligence information"). As this report is being written, the scope and the nature of precisely how federal agencies have complied with various portions of FISA are under investigation.

A number of other statutes are designed to provide notification in the event that important information is compromised. If such information is personally identifiable, data breach laws generally require notification of the individuals with whom such information is associated. Federal securities law (the Securities Act of 1933 and the Securities Exchange Act of 1934) requires firms to disclose to investors timely, comprehensive, and accurate information about risks and events that is important to an investment decision. Under this authority, the Securities and Exchange Commission's Division of Corporation Finance in 2011 provided voluntary guidance to firms regarding their obligations to disclose information relating to cybersecurity risks and cyber incidents.[18]

Several federal statutes assign responsibility within the federal government for various aspects of cybersecurity, including the Computer Security Act of 1987 (National Institute of Standards and Technology [NIST], responsible for developing security standards for non-national-security federal computer systems); the Paperwork Reduction Act of 1995 (Office of Management and Budget [OMB], responsible for developing cybersecurity policies); the Clinger-Cohen Act of 1996 (agency heads responsible for ensuring the adequacy of agency information-security policies and procedures); the Homeland Security Act of 2002 (HSA; Department of Homeland Security [DHS], responsible for cybersecurity for homeland security and critical infrastructure); the Cyber Security Research and Development Act of 2002 (NSF and NIST, research responsibilities in cybersecurity); and the Federal Information Security Management Act of 2002 (FISMA; clarified and strengthened NIST and agency cybersecurity responsibilities, established a central federal incident center, and made OMB, rather than the Secretary of Commerce, responsible for promulgating federal cybersecurity standards).

Finally, national security law may affect how the United States may itself use cyber operations in an offensive capacity for damaging adversary information technology systems or the information therein. For example, the War Powers Act of 1973 restricts presidential authority to use the U.S. armed forces in potential or actual hostilities without congressio-

---

[18] U.S. Securities and Exchange Commission, Division of Corporation Finance, "CF Disclosure Guidance: Topic No. 2—Cybersecurity," October 13, 2011, available at http://www.sec.gov/divisions/corpfin/guidance/cfguidance-topic2.htm.

nal authorization. However, the War Powers Act was passed in 1973—that is, at a time that cyber conflict was not a serious possibility—and the War Powers Act is poorly suited to U.S. military forces that might engage in active cyber conflict. Also, the Posse Comitatus Act of 1878 places some constraints on the extent to which, if at all, the Department of Defense—within which is resident a great deal of cybersecurity knowledge—can cooperate with civil agencies on matters related to cybersecurity.

International Law

International law does not explicitly address the conduct of hostile cyber operations that cross international boundaries. However, one international agreement—the Convention on Cybercrime—seeks to harmonize national laws that criminalize certain specifically identified computer-related actions or activities, to improve national capabilities for investigating such crimes, and to increase cooperation on investigations.[19] That convention also obliges ratifying states to create laws allowing law enforcement to search and seize computers and "computer data," engage in wiretapping, and obtain real-time and stored communications data, whether or not the crime under investigation is a cybercrime.

International law does potentially touch on hostile cyber operations that cross international boundaries when a hostile cyber operation is the instrumentality through which some regulated action is achieved. A particularly important example of such a case is the applicability of the laws of war (or, equivalently, the law of armed conflict) to cyberattacks. Today, the law of armed conflict is expressed in two legal instruments—the UN Charter and the Geneva and Hague Conventions.

The UN Charter is the body of treaty law that governs when a nation may engage in armed conflict. Complications and uncertainty regarding how the UN Charter should be interpreted with respect to cyberattacks result from three fundamental facts:

- The UN Charter was written in 1945, long before the notion of cyberattacks was even imagined. Thus, the framers of the charter could not have imagined how it might apply to cyber conflict.
- The UN Charter does not define key terms, such as "use of force," "threat of force," or "armed attack." Definitions and meanings can only be inferred from historical precedent and practice, and there are no such precedents for their meaning in the context of cyber conflict.

---

[19] Drafted by the Council of Europe in Strasbourg, France, the convention is available on the Web site of the Council of Europe at http://conventions.coe.int/Treaty/en/Treaties/Html/185.htm.

- The charter is in some ways internally inconsistent. It bans certain acts (uses of force) that could damage persons or property, but allows other acts (economic sanctions) that could damage persons or property. Offensive cyber operations may well magnify such inconsistencies.

The Geneva and Hague Conventions regulate how a nation engaged in armed conflict must behave. These conventions embody several principles, such as the principle of nonperfidy (military forces cannot pretend to be legally protected entities, such as hospitals); the principle of proportionality (the military advantage gained by a military operation must not be disproportionate to the collateral damage inflicted on civilian targets); and the principle of distinction (military operations may be conducted only against "military objectives" and not against civilian targets). But as with the UN Charter, the Geneva Conventions are silent on cyberattack as a modality of conflict, and how to apply the principles mentioned above in any instance involving cyber conflict may be uncertain in some cases.

A second important example of an implicit relationship between hostile cyber operations and international law is that of cyber exploitation by one nation to acquire intelligence information from another. Espionage is an illegal activity under the domestic laws of virtually all nations, but not under international law. There are no limits in international law on the methods of collecting information, what kinds of information can be collected, how much information can be collected, or the purposes for which collected information may be used.

As noted above, international law is also articulated through customary international law—that is, the general and consistent practices of states followed from a sense of legal obligation. Such law is not codified in the form of treaties but rather is found in international case law. Here too, guidance for what counts as proper behavior in cyberspace is lacking. Universal adherence to norms of behavior in cyberspace could help to provide nations with information about the intentions and capabilities of other adherents, in both strategic and tactical contexts, but there are no such norms today.

Foreign Domestic Law

Foreign nations are governed by their own domestic laws that relate to cybersecurity. When another nation's laws criminalize similar bad activities in cyberspace, the United States and that other nation are more likely to be able to work together to combat hostile cyber operations that cross their national borders. For example, the United States and China have been able to find common ground in working together to combat the production of child pornography and spam.

But when security- or privacy-related laws of different nations are inconsistent, foreign law often has an impact on the ability of the United States to trace the origin of hostile cyber operations against the United States or to take action against perpetrators under another nation's jurisdiction. Legal dissimilarities have in the past impeded both investigation and prosecution of hostile cyber operations that have crossed international boundaries.

4.2.4 Organizational Purview

From an organizational perspective, the response of the United States to a hostile operation in cyberspace by a nonstate actor is often characterized as depending strongly on whether that operation is one that requires a law enforcement response or a national security response. This characterization is based on the idea that a national security response relaxes many of the constraints that would otherwise be imposed on a law enforcement response. For example, active defense—either by active threat neutralization or by cyber retaliation—may be more viable under a national security response paradigm, whereas a law enforcement paradigm might call for strengthened passive defense measures to mitigate the immediate threat and other activities to identify and prosecute the perpetrators.

When a cyber incident first occurs, its scope and nature are not likely to be clear, and many factors relevant to a decision will not be known. For example, because cyber weapons can act over many time scales, anonymously, and clandestinely, knowledge about the scope and character of a cyberattack will be hard to obtain quickly. Attributing the incident to a nation-state or to a non-national actor may not be possible for an extended period of time. Other nontechnical factors may also play into the assessment of a cyber incident, such as the state of political relations with other nations that are capable of launching the cyber operations involved in the incident.

Once the possibility of a cyberattack is made known to national authorities, information must be gathered to determine perpetrator and purpose, and must be gathered using the available legal authorities. Some entity within the federal government integrates the relevant information, and then it or another higher entity (e.g., the National Security Council) renders a decision about next steps to be taken, and in particular whether a law enforcement or national security response is called for.

How might some of the factors described above be taken into account as a greater understanding of the event develops? Law enforcement equities are likely to predominate in the decision-making calculus if the scale of the attack is small, if the assets targeted are not important military assets or elements of critical infrastructure, or if the attack has not created substantial damage. However, an incident with sufficiently serious consequences (e.g., death and/or significant destruction) that it would qualify as a use of force or an armed attack on the United States had it been carried out with kinetic means would almost certainly be regarded as a national security matter. Other factors likely to influence such a determination are the geographic origin of the attack and the nature of the party responsible for the attack (e.g., national government, terrorist group).

U.S. law has traditionally drawn distinctions between authorities granted to law enforcement (Title 18 of the U.S. Code), the Department of Defense (Title 10 of the U.S. Code), and the intelligence community (Title 50 of the U.S. Code), but in an era of international terrorist threats, these distinctions are not as clear in practice as when threats to the United States emanated primarily from other nations. That is, certain threats to the United States implicate both law enforcement and national security equities and call for a coordinated response by all relevant government agencies.

When critical infrastructure is involved, the entity responsible for integrating the available information and recommending next steps to be taken has evolved over time. Today, the National Cybersecurity and Communications Integration Center (NCCIC) is the cognizant entity within the U.S. government that fuses information on the above factors and integrates the intelligence, national security, law enforcement, and private-sector equities regarding the significance of any given cyber incident.[20]

Whatever the mechanisms for aggregating and integrating information related to a cyber incident, the function served is an essential one—and if the relationships, the communications pathways, the protocols for exchanging data, and the authorities are not established and working well in advance, responses to a large unanticipated cyber incident will be uncoordinated and delayed.

4.2.5 Deterrence

Deterrence relies on the idea that inducing a would-be intruder to refrain from acting in a hostile manner is as good as successfully defending against or recovering from a hostile cyber operation. Deterrence through the threat of retaliation is based on imposing negative consequences on adversaries for attempting a hostile operation.

Imposing a penalty on an intruder serves two functions. It serves

---

[20] See U.S. Department of Homeland Security, "About the National Cybersecurity and Communications Integration Center," available at http://www.dhs.gov/about-national-cybersecurity-communications-integration-center.

the goal of justice—an intruder should not be able to cause damage with impunity, and the penalty is a form of punishment for the intruder's misdeeds. In addition, it sets the precedent that misdeeds can and will result in a penalty for the intruder, and it seeks to instill in future would-be intruders the fear that he or she will suffer from any misdeeds they might commit, and thus to deter such action, thereby discouraging further misdeeds.

What the nature of the penalty should be and who should impose the penalty are key questions in this regard. (Note that a penalty need not take the same form as the hostile action itself.) What counts as a sufficient attribution of hostile action to a responsible party is also a threshold issue, because imposing penalties on parties not in fact responsible for a hostile action has many negative ramifications.

For deterrence to be effective, the penalty must be one that affects the adversary's decision-making process and changes the adversary's cost-benefit calculus. Possible penalties in principle span a broad range, including jail time, fines, or other judicially sanctioned remedies; damage to or destruction of the information technology assets used by the perpetrator to conduct a hostile cyber operation; loss of or damage to other assets that are valuable to the perpetrator; or other actions that might damage the perpetrator's interests.

But the appropriate choice of penalty is not separate from the party imposing the penalty. For example, the prospect that the victim of a hostile operation might undertake destructive actions against a perpetrator raises the spectre of vigilantism and easily leads to questions of accountability and/or disproportionate response.

Law enforcement authorities and the judicial system rely on federal and state law to provide penalties, but they presume the existence of a process in which a misdeed is investigated, perpetrators are prosecuted, and if found guilty are subject to penalties imposed by law. As noted in Section 4.2.3, a number of laws impose penalties for the willful conduct of hostile cyber operations. Deterrence in this context is based on the idea that a high likelihood of imposing a significant penalty for violations of such laws will deter such violations.

In a national security context, when the misdeed in question affects national security, the penalty can take the form of diplomacy such as demarches and breaks in diplomatic relations, economic actions such as trade sanctions, international law enforcement such as actions taken in international courts, nonkinetic military operations such as deploying forces as visible signs of commitment and resolve, military operations such as the use of cruise missiles against valuable adversary assets, or cyber operations launched in response.

In a cyber context, the efficacy of deterrence is an open question.

Deterrence was and is a central construct in contemplating the use of nuclear weapons and in nuclear strategy—because effective defenses against nuclear weapons are difficult to construct, using the threat of retaliation to persuade an adversary to refrain from using nuclear weapons is regarded by many as the most plausible and effective alternative to ineffective or useless defenses. Indeed, deterrence of nuclear threats in the Cold War established the paradigm in which the conditions for successful deterrence are largely met.

It is an entirely open question whether cyber deterrence is a viable strategy. Although nuclear weapons and cyber weapons share one key characteristic (the superiority of offense over defense), they differ in many other key characteristics. For example, it is plausible to assume that a large-scale nuclear attack can be promptly recognized and attributed, but it is not plausible to assume the same for a large-scale cyberattack.

4.3 ASSESSING CYBERSECURITY

How should a system's security be assessed? Cybersecurity analysts have strong intuitions that some systems are more secure than others, but assessing a system's cybersecurity posture turns out to be a remarkably thorny problem. From a technical standpoint, assessing the nature and extent of a system's security is confounded by two factors:

- A system can be secure only to the extent that system designers can precisely specify what it means for the system to operate securely. Indeed, many vulnerabilities in systems can be traced to misunderstandings or a lack of clarity about what a system should do under a particular set of circumstances (such as the use of penetration techniques or attack tools that the defender has never seen before).
- A system that contains functionality that should not be present according to the specifications may be insecure, because that excess functionality may entail doing something harmful. Discovering that a system has "extra" functionality that may be harmful turns out to be an extraordinarily difficult task as a general rule.

Viewing system security from an operational perspective rather than just a technical one shows that security is a holistic, emergent, multidimensional property of a system rather than a fixed attribute. Indeed, many factors other than technology affect the security of a system, including the system's configuration, the cybersecurity training and awareness of the people using the system, the access control policy in place, the boundaries of the system (e.g., are users allowed to connect their own devices to the system?), the reliability of personnel, and the nature of the threat against the system.

Accordingly, a discussion cast simply in terms of whether a system is or is not secure is almost certainly misleading. Assessing the security of a system must include qualifiers such as, Security against what kind of threat? Under what circumstances? For what purpose? With what configuration? Under what security policy?

What does the discussion above imply for the development of cybersecurity metrics—measurable quantities whose value provides information about a system or network's resistance to a hostile cyber operation? Metrics are intended to help individuals and companies make rational quantitative decisions about whether or not they have "done enough" with respect to cybersecurity. These parties would be able to quantify cost-benefit tradeoffs in implementing security features, and they would be able to determine if System A is more secure than System B. Good cybersecurity metrics would also support a more robust insurance market in cybersecurity founded on sound actuarial principles and knowledge.

The holy grail for cybersecurity analysts is an overall cybersecurity metric that is applicable to all systems and in all operating environments. The discussion above, not to mention several decades' worth of research and operational experience, suggests that this holy grail will not be achieved for the foreseeable future. But other metrics may still be useful under some circumstances.

It is important to distinguish between input metrics (metrics for what system users or designers do to the system), output metrics (metrics for what the system produces), and outcome metrics (metrics for what users or designers are trying to achieve—the "why" for the output metrics).[21]

- Input metrics reflect system characteristics, operation, or environment that are believed to be associated with desirable cybersecurity outcomes. An example of an input metric could be the annual cybersecurity budget of an organization. In practice, many input metrics for cybersecurity are not validated in practice, and/or are established intuitively.
- Output metrics reflect system performance with respect to parameters that are believed to be associated with desirable cybersecurity outcomes. An output metric in a cybersecurity context could be the number of cybersecurity incidents in a given year. Output metrics can often be assessed through the use of a red team. Sometimes known as "white-hat"

---

[21] See Republic of South Africa, "Key Performance Information Concepts," Chapter 3 in *Framework for Managing Programme Performance Information*, National Treasury, Pretoria, South Africa, May 2007, available at http://www.thepresidency.gov.za/learning/reference/framework/part3.pdf.

or "ethical" hackers, a red team attempts to penetrate a system's security under operational conditions with the blessing of senior management, and then reports to senior management on its efforts and what it has learned about the system's security weaknesses. Red teaming is often the most effective way to assess the cybersecurity posture of an organization, because it provides a high-fidelity simulation of a real adversary's actions.

• Outcome metrics reflect the extent to which the system's cyber-security properties actually produce or reflect desirable cybersecurity outcomes. In a cybersecurity context, an outcome measure might be the annual losses for an organization due to cybersecurity incidents.

With the particular examples chosen, a possible logic chain is that an organization that increases its cybersecurity expenditures can reduce the number of cybersecurity incidents and thereby reduce the annual losses due to such incidents. Of course, if an organization spends its cyberse-curity budget unwisely, the presumed relationship between budget and number of incidents may well not hold.

Also, the correlation between improvement in a cybersecurity input metric and better cybersecurity outcomes may well be disrupted by an adaptive adversary. The benefit of the improvement may endure, how-ever, against adversaries that do not adapt—and thus the resulting cyber-security posture against the entire universe of threats may in fact be improved.

4.4 ON THE NEED FOR RESEARCH

Within each of the approaches for improving cybersecurity described above, research is needed in two broad categories. First, problem-specific research is needed to find good solutions for pressing cybersecurity prob-lems. A good solution to a cybersecurity problem is one that is effective, is robust against a variety of attack types, is inexpensive and easy to deploy, is easy to use, and does not significantly reduce or cripple other function-ality in the system of which it is made a part. Problem-specific research includes developing new knowledge on how to improve the prospects for deployment and use of known solutions to given problems.

Second, even assuming that everything known today about improv-ing cybersecurity was immediately put into practice, the resulting cyber-security posture—although it would be stronger and more resilient than it is now—would still be inadequate against today's high-end threat, let alone tomorrow's. Closing this gap—a gap of knowledge—will require substantial research as well.

Several principles, described in the 2007 NRC report *Toward a Safer and More Secure Cyberspace*, should shape the cybersecurity research agenda:

- *Conduct cybersecurity research as though its application will be important.* The scope of cybersecurity research must extend to understanding how cybersecurity technologies and practice can be applied in real-life contexts. Consequently, fundamental research in cybersecurity will embrace organizational, sociological, economic, legal, and psychological factors as well as technological ones.

- *Hedge against uncertainty in the nature and severity of the future cybersecurity threat.* A balance in the research portfolio between research addressing low-end and high-end threats is necessary. Operationally, it means that the R&D agenda in cybersecurity should be both broader and deeper than might be required if only low-end threats were at issue. (Because of the long lead time for large-scale deployments of any measure, part of the research agenda must include research directed at reducing those long lead times.)

- *Ensure programmatic continuity.* A sound research program should also support a substantial effort in research areas with a long time horizon for payoff. This is not to say that long-term research cannot have intermediate milestones, although such milestones should be treated as midcourse corrections rather than "go/no-go" decisions that demoralize researchers and make them overly conservative. Long-term research should engage both academic and industry actors, and it can involve collaboration early and often with technology-transition stakeholders, even in the basic science stages.

- *Respect the need for breadth in the research agenda.* Cybersecurity risks will be on the rise for the foreseeable future, but few specifics about those risks can be known with high confidence. Thus, it is not realistic to imagine that one or even a few promising approaches will prevent or even substantially mitigate cybersecurity risks in the future, and cybersecurity research must be conducted across a broad front. In addition, because qualitatively new attacks can appear with little warning, a broad research agenda is likely to decrease significantly the time needed to develop countermeasures against these new attacks when they appear. Priorities are still important, but they should be determined by those in a position to respond most quickly to the changing environment—namely, the research constituencies that provide peer review and the program managers of the various research-supporting agencies. Notions of breadth and diversity in the cybersecurity research agenda should themselves be interpreted broadly as well, and might well be integrated into other research programs such as software and systems engineering, operating systems, programming languages, networks, Web applications, and so on.

- *Disseminate new knowledge and artifacts (e.g., software and hardware prototypes) to the research community.* Dissemination of research results beyond one's own laboratory is necessary if those results are to have a wide impact—a point that argues for cybersecurity research to be conducted on an unclassified basis as much as possible. Other information to be shared as widely as possible includes threat and incident information that can help guide future research.

As for the impact of research on the nation's cybersecurity posture, it is not reasonable to expect that research alone will make any substantial difference at all. Indeed, many factors must be aligned if research is to have a significant impact. Specifically, IT vendors must be willing to regard security as a product attribute that is coequal with performance and cost; IT researchers must be willing to value cybersecurity research as much as they value research into high-performance or cost-effective computing; and IT purchasers must be willing to incur present-day costs in order to obtain future benefits.

5

Tensions Between Cybersecurity and Other Public Policy Concerns

As noted in Chapter 1, progress in public policy to improve the nation's cybersecurity posture has not been as rapid as might have been expected. One reason—perhaps the most important reason—is that cybersecurity is only one of a number of significant public policy issues—and measures taken to improve cybersecurity potentially have negative effects in these other areas. This chapter elaborates on some of the most significant tensions.

5.1 ECONOMICS

Economics and cybersecurity are intimately intertwined in the public policy debate in two ways—the scale of economic losses due to adversary operations for cyber exploitation and the effects of economics on the scope and nature of vendor and end-user investments in cybersecurity. (To date, the economic losses due to cyberattack are negligible by comparison.)

5.1.1 Economic Approaches to Enhancing Cybersecurity

As implied in Chapter 4, economic approaches to promote cybersecurity should identify actions that lower barriers and eliminate disincentives. They should create incentives to boost the economic benefits that flow from attention to cybersecurity and should penalize inattention to cybersecurity or actions that cause harm in cyberspace. Some of the possible approaches are described briefly below, although there is no clear national consensus on which of these, if any, should be implemented as policy, and legislation has not been passed on any of these approaches.

- *Use of existing market mechanisms but with improved flow of information.*
  — One type of information is more and better information about threats and vulnerabilities, which could enable individual organizations to take appropriate action to strengthen their cybersecurity postures. For example, an organization may be driven to action if it hears that a large number of other organizations have already fallen victim to a given threat.
  — A second type of information is information about an individual organization's cybersecurity posture. For example, individual organizations in particular sectors of the economy can determine and adopt appropriate best-practice cybersecurity measures for those sectors. Another party, such as a government regulatory agency in the case of already-regulated industries, an insurance company for organizations carrying cybersecurity insurance, or the Securities and Exchange Commission for publicly held companies, would audit the adequacy of the organization's adoption of best practices and publicize the results of such audits.[1] Publicity about such results would in principle incentivize these organizations to improve their cybersecurity postures.

- *Insurance.* The insurance industry may have a role in incentivizing better cybersecurity. Consumers that buy insurance to compensate losses incurred because of cybercrime will have lower premiums if they have stronger cybersecurity postures, and thus market forces will help to drive improvements in cybersecurity. A variety of reasons stand in the way of establishing a viable cyber-insurance market: the unavailability of actuarial data to set premiums appropriately; the highly correlated nature of losses from outbreaks (e.g., from viruses) in a largely homogeneous monoculture environment, the difficulty in substantiating claims, the intangible nature of losses and assets, and unclear legal grounds.

- *Standards setting and certification.* This approach is based on three ideas: that good cybersecurity practices can be codified in standards, that such practices actually improve security, and that organizations publicly recognized as conforming to such standards can improve their competitive position in the marketplace. Relevant standards-setting bodies include the National Institute of Standards and Technology for the U.S.

---

[1] President's Council of Advisors on Science and Technology, *Immediate Opportunities for Strengthening the Nation's Cybersecurity,* November 2013, available at http://www.white house.gov/sites/default/files/microsites/ostp/PCAST/pcast_cybersecurity_nov-2013.pdf.

government and the International Organization for Standardization for the private sector.

• *Nonregulatory public-sector mechanisms.* This approach uses some of the tools below to promote greater attention to and action on cybersecurity.

— Procurement regulations can be used to insist that information technology systems delivered to government are more secure. With such systems thus available, vendors might be able to offer them to other customers as well.

— The federal government can choose to do business only with firms that provide adequate cybersecurity in their government work.

— The federal government itself could improve its own cybersecurity practices and offer itself as an example for the rest of the nation.

— A variety of tax incentives might be offered to stimulate greater investment in cybersecurity.

— Public recognition of adherence to high cybersecurity standards—a form of certification—might provide "bragging rights" for a firm that would translate into competitive advantages.

— Voluntary standards setting by government can specify cybersecurity standards if private organizations do not so.

• *Liability.* This approach presumes that vendors and/or system operators held financially responsible for harms that result from cybersecurity breaches will make greater efforts than they do today to reduce the likelihood of such breaches. Opponents argue that the threat of liability would stifle technological innovation, potentially compromise trade secrets, and reduce the competitiveness of products subject to such forces. Moreover, they argue that vendors and operators should not be held responsible for cybersecurity incidents that can result from factors that are not under their control.

• *Direct regulation.* Regulation would be based on enforceable mandates for various cybersecurity measures. This is the ultimate form of changing the business cases—comply or face a penalty. Direct regulation might, for example, call for all regulated institutions to adopt certain kinds of standards relating to cybersecurity "best practices" regarding the services they provide to consumers or their own internal practices. Opponents of direct regulation argue that several factors would make it difficult to determine satisfactory regulations for cybersecurity.[2] For example, regulations might divert resources that would otherwise be used to address actual threats. Costs of implementation would be highly variable and dependent on a number of factors beyond the control of the

---

[2] Alfredo Garcia and Barry Horowitz, "The Potential for Underinvestment in Internet Security: Implications for Regulatory Policy," *Journal of Regulatory Economics* 31(1):37-55, 2007, available at http://ssrn.com/abstract=889071.

regulated party. Risks vary greatly from system to system. There is wide variation in the technical and financial ability of firms to support security measures.

As an example of growing awareness that incentives may be important in cybersecurity, the present administration is promulgating its Cybersecurity Framework. Under development as this report is being written, the framework is a set of core practices to develop capabilities to manage cybersecurity.[3] To encourage critical infrastructure companies to adopt this framework, the administration has identified a number of possible incentives that it is currently exploring, including:[4]

- Special consideration in the awards process for federal critical infrastructure grants;
- Priority in receiving certain government services, such as technical assistance in non-emergency situations;
- Reduced tort liability, limited indemnity, higher burdens of proof to establish liability, or the creation of a federal legal privilege that preempts state disclosure requirements; and
- Public recognition for adopters of the framework.

5.1.2 Economic Impact of Compromises in Cybersecurity

Regarding the negative economic impact of compromises in cybersecurity, numbers as high as $1 trillion annually have been heard in the public debate, and in 2012, the commander of U.S. Cyber Command asserted that the loss of industrial information and intellectual property through cyber espionage constitutes the "greatest transfer of wealth in history."[5] But in point of fact, the uncertainty in the actual magnitude is quite large, and other analysts speculate that the actual numbers—though significant in their own right—might be much lower than the highest known estimates.

For example, loss of intellectual property is today the poster child for

---

[3] National Institute of Standards and Technology, "Executive Order 13636: Cybersecurity Framework," available at http://www.nist.gov/cyberframework/.

[4] Michael Daniel, "Incentives to Support the Adoption of the Cybersecurity Framework," August 6, 2013, available at http://www.whitehouse.gov/blog/2013/08/06/incentives-support-adoption-cybersecurity-framework.

[5] Josh Rogin, "NSA Chief: Cybercrime Constitutes the Greatest Transfer of Wealth in History," July 9, 2012, available at http://thecable.foreignpolicy.com/posts/2012/07/09/nsa_chief_cybercrime_constitutes_the_greatest_ transfer_of_wealth_in_ history#sthash.0k7NmFmQ.dpbs. The methodologies underlying such claims are controversial and are discussed in Section 3.6 on threat assessment.

the negative economic impact of adversarial cyber operations. However, intellectual property is unlike physical property in some very important ways, not the least of which is the fact that "stolen" intellectual property is *still available* to its owner, which can still exercise a considerable degree of control over it. "Stolen" intellectual property is really copied intellectual property, which means that the owner no longer has exclusive control over it. Moreover, valuing intellectual property is a complex process—is the value of intellectual property what it cost to produce that intellectual property, or what it might generate in revenues over its lifetime? How should a reduction in the period of exclusive control be valued? And there is no assurance that a taker of intellectual property will be able to use it properly or effectively.

Uncertainties also apply to valuing the loss of sensitive business information (such as negotiating strategies and company inside information). Company A may want to keep its negotiating strategy confidential, but if Company B, a competitor, knows it, Company B may be able to undercut Company A and unfairly win a contract. Insider information about Company C may lead to stock market manipulation. The loss of a contract is easy to value, but given that many factors usually affect the outcomes of such competitions, how could one tie a competitive loss to the loss of sensitive business information?

Opportunity costs are particularly hard to define. For example, service disruptions often delay service but do not deny it, and a customer who visits a Web site that is inaccessible today may well visit it tomorrow when it is accessible. Should the opportunity cost of a disruption be defined as the business foregone during the disruption or only the business that was lost forever? Damage to the reputation of a victimized company, also a category of opportunity cost, is often temporary—a company suffering a cybersecurity incident that is made public may see its stock price suffer, but a McAfee-CSIS report indicates that such a price drop usually lasts no more than a quarter.[6]

Last, a number of other factors also affect the reliability of various estimates. Companies may not know that they have been victimized by a cyber intrusion. They may know they have been victimized but refrain from reporting it. The surveys taken to determine economic loss are often not representative, and questions about loss can be structured in a way that does not allow erroneously large estimates to be corrected by errors on the other side of the ledger.[7]

---

[6] Center for Strategic and International Studies, *The Economic Impact of Cybercrime and Cyber Espionage*, July 2013, available at http://www.mcafee.com/us/resources/reports/rp-economic-impact-cybercrime.pdf.

[7] Dinei Florencio and Cormac Herley, "Sex, Lies, and Cyber-crime Surveys," available at http://research.microsoft.com/apps/pubs/default.aspx?id=149886.

Estimates of losses due to cybercrime are intended to motivate action to deal with the cybercrime problem, and larger estimates presumably make the problem more urgent for policy makers to address. But disputes about methodology can erode the credibility of demands to take immediate action, even when the lower end of such estimates may be large enough from a public policy standpoint to warrant action.

Perhaps more important, even if the economic losses are large, users of information technology may be making a judgment that such losses are simply a cost of doing business. Although they may be loath to acknowledge it publicly, some users argue that they will not invest in security improvements until the losses they are incurring make such an investment economically worthwhile. Although economic calculations of this nature are unlikely to be the only reason that users fail to invest at a level commensurate with some externally assessed need, it may well be that some of these users simply have a different definition of need.

5.2 INNOVATION

A stated goal of U.S. public policy is to promote innovation in products and services in the private sector. In information technology (as in other fields), vendors have significant financial incentives to gain a first-mover or a first-to-market advantage. For example, the vendor of a useful product or service that is first to market has a virtual monopoly on the offering, at least until a competitor comes along. During this period, the vendor has the chance to establish relationships with customers and to build loyalty, making it more difficult for a competitor to establish itself. Furthermore, customers of the initial product or service may well be reluctant to incur the costs of switching to a competitor.

Policy actions that detract from the ability of the private sector to innovate are inherently suspect from this perspective, and in particular policy actions to promote greater attention to cybersecurity in the private sector often run up against concerns that these actions will reduce innovation. The logic of reducing time to market for information technology products or services runs counter to enhancing security, which adds complexity, time, and cost in design and testing while being hard to value by customers. For example, the real-world software development environment is not conducive to focusing on security from the outset. Software developers often experience false starts, and many "first-try" artifacts are thrown away. In this environment, it makes very little sense to invest up front in that kind of adherence unless such adherence is relatively inexpensive.

Furthermore, to apply secure development principles such as those described in Box 4.2, software designers and architects have to know very well and in some considerable detail just what the ultimate artifact is supposed to do. But some large software systems emerge from incremental additions to small software systems in ways that have not been anticipated by the designers of the original system, and sometimes users change their minds about the features they want, or even worse, want contradictory features.

Functionality that users demand is sometimes in tension with security as well. Users demand attributes such as ease of use, interoperability, and backward compatibility. Often, information technology purchasers (whether individuals or firms) make product choices based on features, ease of use, performance, and dominance in a market, although in recent years the criteria for product selection have broadened to include security to some extent in some business domains.

As an example, consider the choice that a vendor must make in shipping a product—whether to ship with the security features turned on or off. If the purchaser is a novice, he or she may find that security features often get in the way of using the product, an outcome that may lead to frustration and customer dissatisfaction. Inability to use the product may also result in a phone call to the vendor for customer service, which is expensive for the vendor to provide. By contrast, shipping the product with security features turned off tends to reduce one source of customer complaints and makes it easier for the customer to use the product. The customer is likely to realize at a later time the consequences of any security breaches that may occur as a result, at which point tying those consequences to the vendor's decision may be difficult. Under these circumstances, many vendors will chose to ship with security turned off—and many customers will simply accept forever the vendor's initial default settings.

Restricting users' access privileges often has serious usability implications and makes it harder for users to get legitimate work done, as for example when someone needs higher access privileges temporarily but on a time-urgent basis. Program features that enable adversary access can be turned off, but doing so may disable functionality needed or desired by users. In some cases, closing down access paths and introducing cybersecurity to a system's design slows it down or makes it harder to use. Other security measures may make it difficult to get work done or cumbersome to respond quickly in an emergency situation.

At the level of the computer programs needed for an innovative product or service, implementing the checking, monitoring, and recovery needed for secure operation requires a lot of computation and does not come for free. In addition, user demands for backward compatibility at the applications level often call for building into new systems some of the same security vulnerabilities present in the old systems.

5.3 CIVIL LIBERTIES

Policy at the nexus of cybersecurity and civil liberties often generates substantial controversy. Civil liberties have an important informational dimension to them, and cybersecurity is in large part about protecting information, so it is not surprising that measures taken to enhance cybersecurity might raise civil liberties concerns.

5.3.1 Privacy

Privacy is an ill-defined concept in the sense that people use the term to mean many different things, but it resists a clear, concise definition because it is experienced in a variety of social contexts. In the context of information, the term "privacy" usually refers to making ostensibly private information about an individual unavailable to parties who should not have that information. Privacy interests attach to the gathering, control, protection, and use of information about individuals.

Privacy and cybersecurity intersect in a number of ways, although the security of information against unauthorized access is different than privacy.[8] In one basic sense, cybersecurity measures can protect privacy—an intruder seeking ostensibly private information (e.g., personal e-mails or photographs, financial or medical records, phone calling records) may be stymied by good cybersecurity measures.

But certain measures taken to enhance cybersecurity can also violate privacy. For example, some proposals call for technical measures to block Internet traffic containing malware before it reaches its destination. But to identify malware-containing traffic, the content of *all* in-bound network traffic must be inspected. But inspection of traffic by any party other than its intended recipient is regarded by some as a violation of privacy, because most traffic will in fact be malware-free. Under many circumstances, inspection of traffic in this manner is also a violation of law.

Another measure for enhancing cybersecurity calls for sharing technical information on various kinds of traffic with entities responsible for identifying and responding to intrusions. Technical information is information associated directly with the mechanisms used to effect access, to take advantage of vulnerabilities, or to execute malware payloads. For example:

---

[8] What an individual regards as "private" may not be the same as what the law designates as being worthy of privacy protection—an individual may believe a record of pre-existing medical conditions should be kept away from life insurance providers, but the law may say otherwise. No technical security measure will protect the privacy interests of those who believe that legally authorized information flows constitute a violation of privacy.

- *Malware (or intrusion) signatures.* Sharing such information could help installations identify malware before it has a chance to affect vulnerable systems or networks.
- *Time-correlated information on intrusions.* Such information is an essential aspect of attack assessment, because simultaneous intrusions on multiple installations across the nation might signal the onset of a major attack. Important installations thus must be able to report their status to authorities responsible for coordinating such information.
- *Frequency, nature, and effect of intrusions.* How often are intrusions of a given type occurring? What tools are they using? What is the apparent purpose of these intrusions?

In some cases, real-time or near-real-time information sharing is a prerequisite for a prompt response. In other cases, after-the-fact coordination of information from multiple sources is necessary for forensic purposes or for detecting similar intrusions in the future. Nonetheless, many organizations are hesitant to share such information, raising concerns about possible antitrust or privacy violations and loss of advantages with respect to their competitors. Private-sector organizations are also sometimes reluctant to share such information with government agencies, for fear of attracting regulatory attention. Similar issues also arise regarding the sharing of threat information among agencies of the U.S. government, especially those within the intelligence community. The result can be that a particular method of intrusion may be known to some (e.g., elements of the intelligence community or the military) and unknown to others (e.g. industry and the research community), thus impeding or delaying the development of effective countermeasures.

In addition, privacy rights can be implicated if the definition of the information to be shared is cast too broadly, if personally identifiable information is not removed from the information to be shared, or if the scope of the allowed purposes for sharing information goes beyond matters related to cybersecurity. The essential privacy point is that systematically obtaining the information described above for hostile traffic requires inspection of *all* incoming traffic, most of which is not relevant or hostile in any way. If the entities with whom the information is shared are law enforcement or national security authorities, privacy concerns are likely to be even stronger.

5.3.2 Free Expression

Freedom of expression, which includes freedom of religion, freedom of speech, freedom of the press, freedom of assembly, and freedom to petition the government, encompasses civil liberties that are often infringed when the causes involved are unpopular. In such cases, one way of protecting individuals exercising rights of free expression is to provide a means for them to do so anonymously. Thus, an individual may choose to participate in an unattributable online discussion that is critical of the government or of an employer, to make an unidentified financial contribution to an organization or a political campaign, to attend a meeting organized by unpopular groups, or to write an unattributed article expressing a politically unpopular point of view.

Civil liberties concerns regarding free expression attach primarily to strong authentication at the packet level. Few people object to online banks using strong authentication—but many have strong objections to mandatory strong authentication that is independent of the application in question, and in particular they are concerned that strong authentication will curtail their freedom of expression.

To address concerns about free expression, it is sometimes proposed that mandatory strong authentication should apply to a second Internet, which would be used by critical infrastructure providers and others who preferred to operate in a strongly authenticated environment. Although a new network with such capabilities would indeed help to identify attackers under some circumstances, attackers would nevertheless invariably seek other ways to counter the authentication capabilities of this alternative, such as compromising the machines connected to the new network.[9]

In addition, a new network may come with a number of drawbacks, such as retaining the economies of the present-day Internet and preventing any connection, physical or logical, to the regular Internet through which cyberattacks might be launched. On this last point, experience with large networks indicates that maintaining an actual air-gap isolation between two Internets would be all but impossible—not for technical reasons but because of a human tendency to make such connections for the sake of convenience.

5.3.3 Due Process

An important element of protecting civil liberties is due process—the state cannot deprive individuals of civil liberties in the absence of due process. Some cybersecurity measures can put pressure on due process. For example, due process could be compromised if government authorities surveil Internet traffic for cybersecurity purposes in ways that are illegal under existing law or if they cause collateral damage to innocent civilians in the process of responding to an adversarial cyber operation.

---

[9] Steven M. Bellovin, "Identity and Security," *IEEE Security and Privacy* 8(2, March-April):88, 2010.

Also, it is often alleged that responses to cyber intrusions must happen very rapidly—in a matter of milliseconds—because the intrusions occur very rapidly. Leaving aside the question of whether a rapid response is in fact required in all circumstances, even those situations in which a rapid response *is* necessary raise the question of whether due process can be exercised in such a short time. Some tasks, such as high-confidence attribution of a cyber intrusion to the legally responsible actor, may simply be impossible to accomplish in a short time, and yet accomplishment of these tasks may be necessary elements of due process.

5.4 INTERNATIONAL RELATIONS AND NATIONAL SECURITY

5.4.1 Internet Governance

In the international environment of the Internet, "Internet governance" is not a well-defined term. There is broad agreement that Internet governance includes management and coordination of the technical underpinnings of the Internet such as the Domain Name System, and development of the standards and protocols that enable the Internet to function.[10] A more expansive definition of Internet governance, for which there is not broad international agreement, would include matters such as controlling spam; dealing with use of the Internet for illegal purposes; resolving the "digital divide" between developed and developing countries; protecting intellectual property other than domain names; protecting privacy and freedom of expression; and facilitating and regulating e-commerce.[11]

International debates over what should constitute the proper scope of Internet governance are quite contentious, with the United States generally arguing for a very restricted definition and other nations arguing for a more expansive one, and in particular for a definition that includes security from threats in cyberspace.

But different nations have different conceptions of what constitutes a threat from cyberspace. China and Russia, for example, often talk about "information security"—a term that is much more expansive than the U.S. conception of cybersecurity. These nations argue that Internet traffic containing information related to various political developments poses threats to their national security and political stability (e.g., news

---

[10] Lennard G. Kruger, "Internet Governance and the Domain Name System: Issues for Congress," Congressional Research Service, November 13, 2013, available at http://www.fas.org/sgp/crs/misc/R42351.pdf.

[11] National Research Council, *Signposts in Cyberspace: The Domain Name System and Internet Navigation*, The National Academies Press, Washington, D.C., 2005.

stories about corruption at high levels of government) and thus that Internet governance should recognize their rights to manage—and if necessary, block—such traffic, just as other nations would be allowed to block malware-containing traffic. The United States and many Western nations have opposed such measures in multiple forums, and in particular have opposed attempts to broaden the Internet governance agenda in this manner. In this context, disputes over Internet governance are thus often disputes over content regulation in the name of Internet security.

There is also contention about who defines the protocols and standards for passing information and what these protocols and standards should contain, because these protocols and standards affect how traffic can be monitored or controlled. Of particular significance are parties—both in other nations and in the United States—that would require packet-level authentication in the basic Internet protocols in the name of promoting greater security. Requiring authentication in this manner would implicate all of the civil liberties issues discussed above as well as the performance and feasibility issues discussed in Chapter 2.

5.4.2 Reconciling Tensions Between Cybersecurity and Surveillance

As is true for all nations, the United States has multiple policy objectives in cyberspace. For example, the United States is on record as promoting cybersecurity internationally, as illustrated in the 2011 White House *International Strategy for Cyberspace*, a document stating that "assuring the free flow of information, *the security and privacy of data* [emphasis added], and the integrity of the interconnected networks themselves are all essential to American and global economic prosperity, security, and the promotion of universal rights."[12]

The United States also collects information around the world for intelligence purposes, and much of such collection depends on the penetration of information technology systems and networks to access the information transiting through them. Cybersecurity measures taken by the users, owners, and operators of these systems and networks thus tend to frustrate intelligence collection efforts, and according to public reports, the United States has undertaken a variety of efforts to circumvent or weaken these measures.

---

[12] White House, *International Strategy for Cyberspace: Prosperity, Security, and Openness in a Networked World*, May 2011, available at http://www.whitehouse.gov/sites/default/files/rss_viewer/international_strategy_for_cyberspace.pdf.

On the face of it, these two policy objectives are inconsistent with each other—one promotes cybersecurity internationally and the other undermines it. Of course, this would not be the first time that policy makers have pursued mutually incompatible objectives—governments frequently have incompatible objectives. A first response to the existence of incompatible objectives is to acknowledge the tension between them, and to recognize the possibility of tradeoffs—more of one may mean less of another, and the likely operational impact of policy tradeoffs made in different ways must be assessed and compared.

An illustration of this tradeoff is the Communications Assistance for Law Enforcement Act (CALEA) of 1994, which directs the telecommunications industry to design, develop, and deploy systems that support law enforcement requirements for electronic surveillance. Intelligence derived from electronic surveillance of adversaries (including criminals, hostile nations, and terrorists) is an important factor in shaping the U.S. response to adversary activities. But measures taken to facilitate CALEA-like access by authorized parties sometimes have the effect of reducing the security of the systems affected by those measures.[13]

Efforts continue today to introduce means of government access to the infrastructure of electronic communications,[14] and some of these efforts are surreptitious. Regardless of the legality and/or policy wisdom of these efforts, a fundamental tradeoff faces national policy makers—whether reduced security for the communications infrastructure is worth the benefits of gaining and/or continuing access to adversary communications. Note also that benefits from the surveillance of adversary communications may be most obvious in the short term, whereas the costs of reduced security are likely to be felt in the long term. Advocates for maintaining government access to adversary communications in this manner will argue that the benefits are large and that whatever reductions in security result from "designed-in" government access are not significant. Opponents of this approach will argue the reverse.

---

[13] An example is provided in Vassilis Prevelakis and Diomidis Spinellis, "The Athens Affair," *IEEE Spectrum* 44(7):26-33, June 29, 2007, available at http://spectrum.ieee.org/telecom/security/the-athens-affair.

[14] See, for example, Susan Landau, "Making Sense from Snowden: What's Significant in the NSA Surveillance Revelations," *IEEE Security and Privacy* 11(4, July/August):54-63, 2013, available at http://www.computer.org/cms/Computer.org/ComputingNow/pdfs/MakingSenseFromSnowden-IEEESecurityAndPrivacy.pdf, and "Making Sense of Snowden, Part II: What's Significant in the NSA Revelations," *IEEE Security and Privacy* 12(1, January/February):62-64, 2014, available at http://doi.ieeecomputersociety.org/10.1109/MSP.2013.161.

5.4.3 Norms of Behavior in Cyberspace

International norms of behavior are intended to guide states' actions, sustain partnerships, and support the rule of law.[15] Norms of international behavior are established in many ways, including the customary practice and behavior of nations and explicit agreements (treaties) that codify behavior that is permitted or proscribed.

The U.S. *International Strategy for Cyberspace* states that in cyberspace, the United States supports the development of a variety of norms for upholding fundamental freedoms; respect for property; valuing privacy; protection from crime; right of self-defense; global interoperability; network stability; reliable access; multi-stakeholder governance; and cybersecurity due diligence. But even a casual inspection of this set of possible norms would suggest that an international consensus for these norms would not be easy to achieve.

One of the most important factors influencing the adoption and enforcement of norms is the ability of all parties to monitor the extent to which other parties are in fact complying with them—parties can flout norms without consequence if they cannot be associated with such behavior. As discussed in Chapter 4 (Box 4.1), attributing actions in cyberspace to an appropriately responsible actor is problematic under many circumstances, especially if prompt attribution is required. Difficulties in attribution are likely to increase the difficulty of establishing norms of behavior in cyberspace.

For illustrative purposes, two domains in which norms may be relevant to cybersecurity relate to conducting cyber operations for different purposes and reaching explicit agreements internationally regarding acceptable and unacceptable behavior.

Distinguishing Between Cyber Operations Conducted for Different Purposes

In the cybersecurity domain, norms of behavior are contentious as well. For example, the United States draws a sharp line between collecting information related to national security and foreign policy and collecting information related to economic and business interests, arguing that the first constitutes espionage (an activity that is not illegal under international law) and that the second constitutes theft of intellectual property and trade secrets for economic advantage.

---

[15] White House, *International Strategy for Cyberspace—Prosperity, Security, and Openness in a Networked World,* May 2011, available at http://www.whitehouse.gov/sites/default/files/rss_viewer/international_strategy_for_cyberspace.pdf.

Most other nations do not draw such a sharp line between these two kinds of information collection. But even were all nations to agree in principle that such a line should be drawn, how might these two types of information (information related to national security and information related to economic and business interests) be distinguished in practice? For instance, consider the plans for a new fighter plane designed for export. Should expropriation of such plans be regarded as an intelligence collection or as theft of intellectual property? If the nature of the information is not sufficient to categorize it, what other characteristics might differentiate it? Where it is stored? What it is used for? All of these questions, and others, remain to be answered.

And a further policy debate remains to be settled. Should the United States maintain the distinction between national security information and information related to economic or business interests? What would be the advantages and disadvantages, if any, to the United States of abandoning this distinction?

Today, the United States does not target intelligence assets for the specific purpose of enhancing the competitive position of U.S. industries or specific U.S. companies. The case for this current policy is based largely on the desire of the United States to uphold a robust legal regime for the protection of intellectual property and for a level playing field to enable competitors from different countries to make their best business cases on their merits. Revising this policy would call for relaxation of the current restraints on U.S. policy regarding intelligence collection for the benefit of private firms, thus allowing such firms to obtain competitively useful and proprietary information from the U.S. intelligence community about the future generations of foreign products, such as airplanes or automobiles, or about business operations and contract negotiating positions of their competitors.

Such a change in policy would require the U.S. government to wrestle with many thorny questions. For example, the U.S. government would have to decide which private firms should benefit from the government's activities, and even what entities should count as a "U.S. firm." U.S. government at the state and local level might well find that the prospect of U.S. intelligence agencies being used to help private firms would not sit well with foreign companies that they were trying to persuade to relocate to the United States. And that use of its intelligence agencies might well undercut the basis on which the United States could object to other nations conducting such activities for the benefit of their own domestic industries and lead to a "Wild West" environment in which anything goes.

Another problematic issue is the difference between cyber exploitation and cyberattack. As noted in Chapter 3, cyber exploitations and cyberattacks use the same approaches to penetrating a system or network; this similarity between exploitations and attacks means that even if an intrusion is detected, the underlying intent may not be clear until some time has passed. Given that the distinction between an attack and an exploitation could be highly consequential, how should the United States respond when it is faced with a cyber intrusion of unknown intent?

For example, consider a scenario in which Elbonia plants software agents in some critical military networks of the United States to collect intelligence information. These agents are designed to be reprogrammable in place—that is, Elbonia can update these agents with new capabilities. During a time of crisis, U.S. authorities discover some of these agents and learn that they have been present for a while, that they are sending back to Elbonia very sensitive information, and that their capabilities can be changed on a moment's notice. Even if no harmful action has yet been taken, it is entirely possible that the United States would see itself as being the target of an impending Elbonian cyberattack.

The possibility of confusion also applies if the United States conducts an exploitation against another nation. If the intent of an exploitation is nondestructive, how—if at all—should the United States inform the other nation of its nondestructive intentions? Such considerations are particularly important during periods of crisis or tension. During such periods, military action may be more likely, and it is entirely plausible that both sides would increase the intensity of the security scans each conducts on its critical systems and networks. More intense security scans often reveal offensive software agents implanted long before the onset of a crisis and that may have been overlooked in ordinary scans, and yet discovery of these agents may well prompt fears that an attack may be impending.[16]

Technical difficulties in distinguishing between exploitations and attack (or preparations for attack) should not preclude the possibility of using other methods for distinguishing them. For example, some analysts suggest that the nature of a targeted entity can provide useful clues to an adversary's intention; others suggest that certain confidence-building measures in cyberspace, such as agreements to refrain from attacking certain kinds of facilities, can help as well. Such questions are open at this time.

---

[16] Herbert Lin, "Escalation Dynamics and Conflict Termination in Cyberspace," *Strategic Studies Quarterly* 6(3):46-70, 2012.

Arms Control in Cyberspace[17]

The intent of an arms control agreement in general is usually to reduce the likelihood that conflict will occur and/or to reduce the destructiveness of any conflict that does occur. Such agreements can be bilateral or multilateral, and they can be cast formally as treaties, informally as memorandums of understanding, or even more informally as coordinated unilateral policies.

In principle, arms control agreements can limit or ban the signatories from conducting some combination of research, development, testing, production, procurement, or deployment on certain kinds of weapons; limit or ban the use of certain weapons and/or the circumstances under which certain weapons may or may not be used; or oblige signatories to take or to refrain from taking certain actions under certain circumstances to reassure other signatories about their benign intent (i.e., to take confidence-building measures).

For cyber weapons (where a cyber weapon is an information technology-based capability for conducting some kind of cyber intrusion), any limit on research, development, testing, production, procurement, or deployment of certain kinds of weapons is unlikely to be feasible. One reason is the verification challenge for such weapons; a second is the fact that such weapons have legitimate uses (e.g., both military and civilian entities use such weapons to test their own defenses). Distinguishing offensive capabilities developed for cyberattack from those used to shore up defenses against cyberattack would seem to be a very difficult if not impossible task.

Restrictions on the use of cyber weapons might entail, as an example, agreement to refrain from launching cyberattacks against national financial systems or power grids, much as nations today have agreed to avoid targeting hospitals in a kinetic attack. Agreements to restrict use are by their nature not verifiable, but the inability to verify such agreements has not prevented the world's nations (including the United States) from agreeing to the Geneva Conventions, which contain similarly "unverifiable" restrictions.

Yet recognizing violations of such agreements may be problematic. One issue is that nonstate actors may have access to some of the same cyber capabilities as do national signatories, and nonstate actors are unlikely to adhere to any agreement that restricts their use of such capabilities. Another issue is the difficulty of tracing cyber intrusions to their

---

[17] Much of the discussion in this section is based on Herbert Lin, "A Virtual Necessity: Some Modest Steps Toward Greater Cybersecurity," *Bulletin of the Atomic Scientists,* September 1, 2012, available at http://www.thebulletin.org/2012/september/virtual-necessity-some-modest-steps-toward-greater-cybersecurity.

ultimate origin. If the ultimate origin of a cyberattack can be concealed successfully, holding the violator of an agreement accountable becomes problematic.

Last, ambiguities between cyber exploitation and cyberattack complicate arms control agreements in cyberspace. A detected act of cyber exploitation may well be assessed by the target as a damaging or destructive act, or at least the prelude to such an act, yet forbidding cyber exploitation would go far beyond the current bounds of international law and fly in the face of what amounts to standard operating procedure today for essentially all nations.

Transparency and confidence-building measures (TCBMs) have been used to promote stability and mutual understanding when kinetic weapons are involved. Some possible TCBMs in cyberspace include (but are not limited to):

- *Incident notification.* Two or more nations agree to notify each other of serious cyber incidents, and to provide each other with information about these incidents.
- *Joint exercises.* Two nations engage in joint exercises to respond to a simulated cyber crisis that affects or involves both nations to see what information each side would need from the other.
- *Publication of declaratory policies and/or doctrine* about how a nation intends to use cyber capabilities, both offensive and defensive, to support its national interests.
- *Notification of relevant nations* regarding certain activities that might be viewed as hostile or escalatory.
- *Direct communication with counterparts* during times of tension or crisis.
- *Mutual cooperation* on matters related to securing cyberspace (e.g., jointly investigating the source of an attack).
- *Imposing on nation-states an obligation* to assist in the investigation and mitigation of cyber intrusions emanating from their territories.

Perhaps the most important challenge to the development of useful TCBMs in cyberspace is that offensive operations fundamentally depend on stealth and deception. Transparency and confidence-building measures are, as the name suggests, intended to be reassuring to an adversary; the success of most offensive operations depends on an adversary being falsely reassured. Thus, the misuse of these measures may well be an element of an adversary's hostile use of cyberspace. In addition, many TCBMs are conventions for behavior (e.g., rules of the road) and as such do not speak to intent—but in cyberspace, intent may be the primary difference between a possibly prohibited act, such as certain kinds of cyberattack, and an allowed one, such as cyber exploitation. Still, examining in a multilateral way various nations' views about the nature of cyber weapons, cyberspace, offensive operations, and so on could promote greater mutual understanding among the parties involved.

Whether the challenges described above convincingly and definitively refute, even in principle, the possibility of meaningful arms control agreements in cyberspace is open to question today. What is clear is that progress in cyber arms control, if it is feasible at all, is likely to be slow.

5.4.4 Managing the Global Supply Chain for Information Technology

The information technology industry is highly globalized. India and China play major roles in the IT industry, and Ireland, Israel, Korea, Taiwan, Japan, and some Scandinavian countries have also developed strong niches within the increasingly globalized industry. Today, a product conceptualized and marketed in the United States might be designed to specifications in Taiwan, and batteries or hard drives obtained from Japan might become parts in a product assembled in China. (Table 5.1 traces possible origins for some components of a laptop computer.) Integrated circuits at the heart of a product might be designed and developed in the United States, fabricated in Taiwan, and incorporated into a

TABLE 5.1 Supply-Chain Geography—An Illustration

Component of Laptop Computer	Location of Facilities Potentially Used by Supplier(s)
Liquid crystal display	China, Czech Republic, Japan, Poland, Singapore, Slovac Republic, South Korea, Taiwan
Memory	China, Israel, Italy, Japan, Malaysia, Philippines, Puerto Rico, Singapore, South Korea, Taiwan, United States
Processor	Canada, China, Costa Rica, Ireland, Israel, Malaysia, Singapore, United States, Vietnam
Motherboard	Taiwan
Hard disk drive	China, Ireland, Japan, Malaysia, Philippines, Singapore, Thailand, United States

SOURCE: U.S. Government Accountability Office, *National Security-Related Agencies Need to Better Address Risks,* GAO-12-361, U.S. Government Printing Office, March 23, 2012, available at http://www.gao.gov/products/GAO-12-361.

product assembled from components supplied from around the world. Similar considerations apply to software—and software is important to any device, component, system, or network.

The global nature of the IT supply chain raises concerns that foreign suppliers may be subject to pressures from their governments to manipulate the supply of critical components of IT systems or networks or, even worse, introduce substandard, faulty, counterfeit, or deliberately vulnerable components into the supply chain. U.S. users of these components, which include both commercial and government entities, would thus be using components that weakened their cybersecurity posture.

To manage the risks associated with a globalized supply chain, users of the components it provides employ a number of strategies, sometimes in concert with each other:[18]

- *Using trusted suppliers*. Such parties must be able to show that they have taken adequate measures to ensure the dependability of the components they supply or ship. Usually, such measures would be regarded as "best practices" that should be taken by suppliers whether they are foreign or domestic.
- *Diversifying suppliers*. The use of multiple suppliers increases the effort that an adversary must exert to be confident of introducing its ersatz components into a particular or specific system of interest.
- *Reducing the time between choosing a supplier and taking possession of the components provided*. A shorter interval reduces the window within which an adversary can develop its ersatz components.
- *Testing components*. Components can be tested to ensure that they live up to the intended performance specifications. However, as a general rule, testing can indicate only the presence of a problem—not its absence. Thus, testing generally cannot demonstrate the presence of unwanted (and hostile) functionality in a component, although testing may be able to provide evidence that the component does in fact perform as it is supposed to perform.

The strategies described above address some of the important process and performance aspects of ensuring the integrity of the IT supply chain. But implementing these strategies entails some cost, and many of the most stringent strategies (e.g., self-fabrication of integrated circuit chips) are too expensive or otherwise impractical for widespread use. It is thus

---

[18] National Institute of Standards and Technology, "NIST Special Publication 800-53—Recommended Security Controls for Federal Information Systems and Organizations," 2010, available at http://csrc.nist.gov/publications/nistpubs/800-53-Rev3/sp800-53-rev3-final_updated-errata_05-01-2010.pdf.

fair to say that the risk associated with corruption in the supply chain can be managed and mitigated to a certain degree—but not avoided entirely.

5.4.5 Role of Offensive Operations in Cyberspace

Policy regarding the use of offensive operations in cyberspace is generally classified. As a matter of logic, it is clear that offensive operations can be conducted for cyber defensive purposes and also for other purposes.[19] Furthermore, according to a variety of public sources, policy regarding offensive operations in cyberspace includes the following points:

- The United States would respond to hostile acts in cyberspace as it would to any other threat to the nation, and reserves the right to use all necessary means—diplomatic, informational, military, and economic—as appropriate and consistent with applicable international law, in order to defend the nation, its allies, its partners, and its interests.[20]
- The laws of war apply to cyberspace,[21] and because the United States has made a commitment to behaving in accordance with these laws, cyber operations conducted by the United States are expected to conform to the laws of war.
- Offensive operations in cyberspace offer "unique and unconventional capabilities to advance U.S. national objectives around the world with little or no warning to the adversary or target and with potential effects ranging from subtle to severely damaging."[22]
- Offensive operations likely to have effects in the United States require presidential approval, except in emergency situations.[23]
- Cyber operations, including offensive operations, that are likely to result in significant consequences (such as loss of life; actions in response against the United States; damage to property; serious adverse foreign policy or economic impacts) require presidential approval.[24]

---

[19] National Research Council, *Technology, Policy, Law, and Ethics Regarding U.S. Acquisition and Use of Cyberattack Capabilities*, The National Academies Press, Washington, D.C., 2009.

[20] White House, *International Strategy for Cyberspace—Prosperity, Security, and Openness in a Networked World*, May 2011, available at http://www.whitehouse.gov/sites/default/files/rss_viewer/international_strategy_for_cyberspace.pdf.

[21] Harold Koh, Speech on International Law on Cyberspace at the USCYBERCOM Inter-Agency Legal Conference, Ft. Meade, Md., September 18, 2012, available at http://opiniojuris.org/2012/09/19/harold-koh-on-international-law-in-cyberspace/.

[22] Robert Gellman, "Secret Cyber Directive Calls for Ability to Attack Without Warning," *Washington Post*, June 7, 2013.

[23] Gellman, "Secret Cyber Directive Calls for Ability to Attack Without Warning," 2013.

[24] Glenn Greenwald and Ewen MacAskill, "Obama Orders U.S. to Draw Up Overseas Target List for Cyberattacks," *The Guardian*, June 7, 2013, available at http://www.theguardian.com/world/2013/jun/07/obama-china-targets-cyber-overseas.

However, despite public knowledge of these points, the United States has not articulated publicly a military doctrine for how cyber capabilities might be used operationally. (As a notable point of comparison, U.S. approaches to using nuclear weapons were publicly discussed during the Cold War.)

A particularly important question about the use of offensive cyber operations is the possibility of escalation, that is, that initial conflict in cyberspace may grow. But the escalation dynamics of conflict in cyberspace are not well understood. How would escalation unfold? How could escalation be prevented (or deterred)? Theories of escalation dynamics, especially in the nuclear domain, are unlikely to apply to escalation dynamics in cyberspace because of the profound differences between the nuclear and cyber domains. Some of the significant differences include the fact that attribution is much more uncertain, the ability of nonstate actors to interfere in the management of a conflict, and the existence of a multitude of states that have nontrivial capabilities to conduct cyber operations.

Last, the fact that the Department of Defense is willing to consider undertaking offensive operations in cyberspace as part of defending its own systems and networks raises the question of whether offensive operations might be useful to defend non-DOD systems, and in particular to defend entities in the private sector. Today, a private-sector entity that is the target of hostile actions in cyberspace can respond to such threats by taking measures within its organizational boundaries to strengthen its defensive posture, and it can seek the assistance of law enforcement authorities to investigate and to take action to mitigate the threat.

Although both of these responses (if properly implemented) are helpful, their effectiveness is limited. Tightening security often reduces important functionality in the systems being locked down—they become more difficult, slower, and inconvenient to use. Sustaining a locked-down posture is also costly. Law enforcement authorities can help, but they cannot do so quickly and the resources they can bring to bear are usually overwhelmed by the demands for their assistance.

A number of commentators and reports have suggested that a more aggressive defensive posture—that is, an active defense—is appropriate under some circumstances.[25] Such an approach, especially if carried out

---

[25] See, for example, Ellen Nakashima, "When Is a Cyberattack a Matter of Defense?," *Washington Post*, February 27, 2012, available at http://www.washington post.com/blogs/checkpoint-washington/post/active-defense-at-center-of-debate-on-cyberattacks/2012/02/27/gIQACFoKeR_blog.html; Ellen Nakashima, "To Thwart Hackers, Firms Salting Their Servers with Fake Data," *Washington Post*, January 2, 2013, available at http://www.washingtonpost.com/world/national-security/to-thwart-hackers-firms-salting-their-servers-with-fake-data/2013/01/02/3ce00712-4afa-11e2-9a42-

by the targeted private-sector entities, raises a host of technical, legal, and policy issues.

A U.S. policy that condones aggressive self-help might serve as a deterrent that reduces the cyber threat to private-sector entities. Alternatively, it might encourage a free-for-all environment in which any aggrieved party anywhere in the world would feel justified in conducting offensive operations against the alleged offender. This debate is not likely to be settled soon.

d1ce6d0ed278_story.html; David E. Sanger and Thom Shanker, "N.S.A. Devises Radio Pathway into Computers," *New York Times*, January 14, 2014, available at http://www. nytimes.com/2014/01/15/us/nsa-effort-pries-open-computers-not-connected-to-internet. html; and Thom Shanker, "U.S. Weighs Its Strategy on Warfare in Cyberspace," *New York Times*, October 19, 2011, available at http://www.nytimes.com/2011/10/19/world/africa/ united-states-weighs-cyberwarfare-strategy.html.

6

Findings and Conclusion

6.1 FINDINGS

Finding 1. Cybersecurity is a never-ending battle. A permanently decisive solution to the problem will not be found in the foreseeable future.

For the most part, cybersecurity problems result from the inherent nature of information technology (IT), the complexity of information technology systems, and human fallibility in making judgments about what actions and information are safe or unsafe from a cybersecurity perspective, especially when such actions and information are highly complex. None of these factors is likely to change in the foreseeable future, and thus there are no silver bullets—or even combinations of silver bullets—that can "solve the problem" permanently.

In addition, threats to cybersecurity evolve. As new defenses emerge to stop older threats, intruders adapt by developing new tools and techniques to compromise security. As information technology becomes more ubiquitously integrated into society, the incentives to compromise the security of deployed IT systems grow. As innovation produces new information technology applications, new venues for criminals, terrorists, and other hostile parties also emerge, along with new vulnerabilities that malevolent actors can exploit. That there are ever-larger numbers of people with access to cyberspace multiplies the number of possible victims and also the number of potential malevolent actors.

Thus, enhancing the cybersecurity posture of a system—and by extension the organization in which it is embedded—must be understood as an ongoing process rather than something that can be done once and then forgotten. Adversaries—especially at the high-end part of the threat spectrum—constantly adapt and evolve their intrusion techniques, and the defender must adapt and evolve as well.

These comments should not be taken to indicate a standstill in the U.S. cybersecurity posture. For example, most major IT vendors have in recent years undertaken significant efforts to improve the security of their products in response to end-user concerns over security. Many of today's products are by many measures more secure than those that preceded these efforts. Support for research in cybersecurity has expanded significantly. And public awareness is greater than it was only a few years ago. Without these efforts, the gap between cybersecurity posture and threat would undoubtedly be significantly greater than it is today, especially with the concurrent rise in the use of IT throughout society.

Ultimately, the relevant policy question is not how the cybersecurity problem can be solved, but rather how it can be made manageable. Societal problems related to the existence of war, terrorism, crime, hunger, drug abuse, and so on are rarely "solved" or taken off the policy agenda once and for all. The salience of such problems waxes and wanes, depending on circumstances, and no one expects such problems to be solved so decisively that they will never reappear—and the same is true for cybersecurity.

Finding 2. Improvements to the cybersecurity posture of individuals, firms, government agencies, and the nation have considerable value in reducing the loss and damage that may be associated with cybersecurity breaches.

If an adversary has the resources to increase the sophistication of its attack and the motivation to keep trying even after many initial attempts fail, it is natural for users to wonder whether it makes sense to bother to improve security at all. Yet, doing nothing until perfect security can be deployed is surely a recipe for inaction that leaves one vulnerable to many lower-level threats.

The value of defensive measures is found in several points:

- Malevolent actors need some time to adapt to defensive measures. During this time, the victim is usually more secure than if no defensive measures had been taken.
- A target often has multiple adversaries, not just one. Even if it is true that adversary A will adapt to new defenses that are raised against A, adversaries B, C, and D may try the same kinds of techniques and tools

that A originally used—these efforts by B, C, and D are likely to be less successful against the target.

- Adaptation is costly, and it forces the adversary to expend resources. Increased difficulty or expense for the adversary sometimes acts as a deterrent of harmful actions.

- Unsuccessful attempts to compromise system security cost the adversary time—and an adversary who works more slowly poses less of a threat than one who works quickly. For example, imposing delays on the adversary may help to prevent him from being able to access everything on the targeted system.

- A well-defended target is usually less attractive to malevolent actors without specific objectives than are poorly defended targets. Thus, if a malevolent actor's objectives do not call for compromising that specific target, he may well move on to a less-well-defended target.

- Certain defensive measures may provide opportunities for the victim to gather intelligence on an intruder's methods and tactics.

- Other defensive measures may enable the victim to know of the adversary's presence and activities, even if the victim is not entirely successful in thwarting the adversary's efforts.

For all of these reasons, efforts to improve cybersecurity postures have significant value.

Finding 3. Improvements to cybersecurity call for two distinct kinds of activity: (a) efforts to more effectively and more widely use what is known about improving cybersecurity, and (b) efforts to develop new knowledge about cybersecurity.

The current U.S. national cybersecurity posture—as it actually is—is determined by knowledge that we have and that we actually use to build a posture that is as robust as we can make it. The gap in security between our national cybersecurity posture and the cyber threat has two essential parts.

The first part—Part 1—of the gap reflects what our cybersecurity posture could be if currently known best cybersecurity practices and technologies were widely deployed and used. Illustrative of things that we know but ignore or have forgotten about, the Part 1 gap is in some sense the difference between the average cybersecurity posture and the best cybersecurity posture possible with known best practices and technologies. The existence of the best is the proof that it is possible to improve the cybersecurity postures that are not the best. The second part—Part 2—is the gap between the strongest posture possible with known practices and technologies and the threat as it exists (and will exist). That is, even if the

Part 1 gap were fully closed, the resulting cybersecurity posture would not be adequate to cope with many of the threats that currently exist, especially the high-end threat.

Improvement to existing technologies and techniques—and indeed the development of entirely new approaches to cybersecurity—is the focus of traditional cybersecurity research. A properly responsive research program is broad and robust, and it addresses both current and possible future threats. Knowledge about new cybersecurity technologies, techniques, tactics, organizational arrangements, and so on will help to strengthen defenses against an ever-evolving threat. Attending to Part 2 of the cybersecurity gap calls for research that targets specific identifiable cybersecurity problems and that also builds a base of technical expertise that increases the ability to respond quickly in the future when threats unknown today emerge.

Note that the Part 1 gap is primarily nontechnical in nature (requiring, e.g., research relating to economic or psychological factors regarding the use of known practices and techniques, enhanced educational efforts to promote security-responsible user behavior, and incentives to build organizational cultures with higher degrees of security awareness). Closing the Part 1 gap does not require new technical knowledge of cybersecurity per se, but rather the application of existing technical knowledge. Research is thus needed to understand how better to promote deployment and use of such knowledge. By contrast, Part 2 of the cybersecurity gap is the domain where new technologies and approaches are primarily relevant and where exploratory technical research is thus important.

Finding 4. Publicly available information and policy actions to date have been insufficient to motivate an adequate sense of urgency and ownership of cybersecurity problems afflicting the United States as a nation.

In 2007, a National Research Council report titled *Toward a Safer and More Secure Cyberspace* called for policy makers to "create a sense of urgency about the cybersecurity problem commensurate with the risks" (p. 229). The report argued that the necessary sense of urgency might be motivated by making publicly available a greater amount of authoritative information about cybersecurity problems and threats and also by changing a decision-making calculus that excessively focuses vendor and end-user attention on the short-term costs of improving their cybersecurity postures.

In the period since that report was issued, the cybersecurity issue has received increasing public attention, and even more authoritative information regarding cybersecurity threats is indeed available publicly. But all too many decision makers still focus on the short-term costs of improving their own organizational cybersecurity postures, and many—even most—people and organizations do not believe that cybersecurity is important enough to warrant any significant change in their own behavior. Furthermore, little has been done to harness market forces to address matters related to the cybersecurity posture of the nation as a whole.

How might things be different if a sense of urgency were in place?

A culture of security would pervade the entire life cycle of IT systems operations, from initial architecture, to design, development, testing, deployment, maintenance, and use. Such a culture would entail, among other things, collaboration among researchers; effective coordination and information sharing between the public and the private sector; the creation of a sufficient core of research specialists necessary to advance the state of the art; the broad-based education of developers, administrators, and users that would make security-conscious practices second nature, just as optimizing for performance or functionality is now, and that would make it easy and intuitive for developers and users to "do the right thing"; the employment of business drivers and policy mechanisms to facilitate security technology transfer and diffusion of R&D into commercial products and services; and the promotion of risk-based decision making (and metrics to support this effort).

Consider what such a culture might mean in practice:

• Developers and designers of IT products and services would use design principles that build security into new products and services, and that focus on security and attack resilience as well as performance and functionality.

• Security would be an integral part of the initial designs for future secure and attack-resilient computer architectures, and it would be integrated into every aspect of the hardware and software design life cycles and research agendas.

• Designers and developers would emphasize defensive design and implementation with the expectation that systems will have to deal with user mistakes and malicious adversaries.

• Security features would be much simpler to use than they are today.

• Designers and developers would assume that systems are insecure until evidence suggests their resistance to compromise.

• End users would be aware of security matters and diligent in their efforts to promote security.

• Senior managers would create organizational cultures in which a high degree of security awareness is the norm, would be willing to accept somewhat lower levels of performance with respect to other organizational goals in order to improve their cybersecurity postures, and would be willing to expend time, energy, talent, and money on cybersecurity.

• Policy makers would be willing to make decisions about tradeoffs that they try to avoid today and would also explain their rationale for those decisions to the nation.

As for market forces and cybersecurity, private-sector entities will not deploy a level of security higher than that which can be justified by today's business cases. In the absence of a market for a higher level of security, vendors will also not provide such security. Accordingly, if the nation's cybersecurity posture is to be improved to a level that is higher than the level to which today's market will drive it, the market calculus that motivates organizations to pay attention to cybersecurity must be altered somehow, and the business cases for the security of these organizations must change.

> **Finding 5. Cybersecurity is important to the United States, but the nation has other interests as well, some of which conflict with the imperatives of cybersecurity. Tradeoffs are inevitable and will have to be accepted through the nation's political and policy-making processes.**

Senior policy makers have many issues on their agenda, and only five issues can be in the top five issues of concern. Even within the national security context, for example, is it more important to attend to nuclear proliferation and terrorism or to rebalancing U.S. military forces to focus on Asia than to address cybersecurity?

Compare, for example, the significance of a nuclear attack on the United States to the significance of a large-scale cyberattack. Despite comparisons that analogize Stuxnet (discussed in Chapter 1) to the use of nuclear weapons at Hiroshima in 1945,[1] one critical difference is that the use of a nuclear weapon provides a very important threshold—there is no sense in which the use of even a single nuclear weapon could be regarded as unimportant or trivial. Indeed, an above-ground nuclear explosion anywhere in the world, especially one that does damage, is unambigu-

---

[1] See, for example, Michael Joseph Gross, "A Declaration of Cyber-War," *Vanity Fair*, April 2011, available at http://www.vanityfair.com/culture/features/2011/04/stuxnet-201104; Alexis C. Madrigal, "Stuxnet Is the Hiroshima of Cyber War," *The Atlantic*, March 4, 2011, available at http://www.theatlantic.com/technology/archive/2011/03/stuxnet-is-the-hiroshima-of-cyber-war/72033/; Mark Clayton, "From the Man Who Discovered Stuxnet, Dire Warnings One Year Later," *Christian Science Monitor*, September 22, 2011, available at http://www.csmonitor.com/USA/2011/0922/From-the-man-who-discovered-Stuxnet-dire-warnings-one-year-later.

ously detectable. By contrast, cyberattacks are often conducted, not necessarily with government sponsorship or approval (although sometimes with government tolerance), by criminals and hackers. Cyber exploitation also occurs on a large scale, often with no one noticing.

But the likelihood of the detonation of a nuclear weapon on U.S. soil is much lower than that of a cyberattack on the United States. So is the nuclear issue, which is more consequential but less likely compared to the cyber issue, worth more attention and effort from policy makers? Or less effort? Both are unquestionably important—but which deserves more action?

Questions of prioritization play heavily in the conduct of foreign relations as well, given that the United States usually has many interests at stake with other nations. For example, the United States has publicly held China and Russia responsible for industrial cyber exploitation on a very large scale. But China is also the largest single holder of U.S. debt and one of the largest trading partners of the United States. China is the single most influential nation with respect to North Korea. The United States and China are arguably the most important nations regarding the mitigation of global climate change. And this list goes on. What is the importance of large-scale cyber exploitation conducted by China for economic advantage relative to other U.S. interests with respect to China? Similar comments hold for Russia as well, although the specifics of U.S. common interests with Russia are different.

The need to manage multiple common interests with China or Russia or any other nation generally requires policy makers to make tradeoffs—pursuing one item on the agenda less vigorously in order to make progress on another item. Moreover, making such tradeoffs almost always results in domestic winners and losers, a fact that makes the losers very unhappy and increases their incentives to make their unhappiness known.

Nor is the competition for policy-maker attention limited to national security and foreign relations. Domestic concerns about unemployment, access to health care, and climate change are also important to the nation, and who is to say whether cybersecurity is a more important problem for the nation to address?

In an environment of many competing priorities, reactive policy making is often the outcome. It is an unfortunate fact of policy and politics that tough decisions are often deferred in the absence of a crisis that forces policy makers to respond. (The same can be true in the private sector as well.) Support for efforts to prevent a disaster that has not yet occurred is typically less than support for efforts to respond to a disaster that has already occurred.

In cybersecurity, this tendency often is reflected in the notion that "no or few attempts have yet been made to compromise the cybersecurity of application X, and why would anyone want to do so anyway?," thus justifying why immediate attention and action to improve the cybersecurity posture of application X can be deferred or studied further. Reactive policy making can be explained in part by the economics of excessive discounting of future events but has many other causes as well.

Progress in cybersecurity policy has also stalled at least in part because of conflicting equities. As a nation, we want better cybersecurity, yes, but we also want a private sector that innovates rapidly, and the convenience of not having to worry about cybersecurity, and the ability for applications to interoperate easily and quickly with one another, and the right to no diminution of our civil liberties, and so on.

But the tradeoffs between security and these other national interests may not be as stark as they might appear at first glance. That is, it may be that the first proposals to advance cybersecurity interests in a given case entail sharper and starker tradeoffs than are necessary and that the second and third proposals may reduce the significance of those tradeoffs. Indeed, proposals may be developed that may advance both interests rather than just one at the expense of another, especially when longer time scales are involved. For example, a properly structured cybersecurity posture for the nation might also provide better protection for intellectual property, thereby enhancing the nation's capability for innovation. More usable security technologies or procedures could provide better security and also increase the convenience of using information technology.

Nonetheless, irreconcilable tensions will sometimes be encountered. At that point, policy makers will have to confront rather than sidestep those tensions, and honest acknowledgment and discussion of the tradeoffs (e.g., a better cybersecurity posture may reduce the nation's innovative capability, may increase the inconvenience of using information technology, may reduce the ability to collect intelligence) will go a long way toward building public support for a given policy position.

Finding 6. The use of offensive operations in cyberspace as an instrument to advance U.S. interests raises many important technical, legal, and policy questions that have yet to be aired publicly by the U.S. government.

As noted in Chapter 5, it is a matter of public record that the United States possesses offensive capabilities in cyberspace, including capabilities for cyber exploitation and for cyberattack. The United States has established U.S. Cyber Command as an entity within the Department of Defense that

> plans, coordinates, integrates, synchronizes and conducts activities to: direct the operations and defense of specified Department of Defense

information networks and prepare to, and when directed, conduct full
spectrum military cyberspace operations in order to enable actions in all
domains, ensure US/Allied freedom of action in cyberspace and deny
the same to our adversaries.[2]

The United States has publicly stated that it does not collect intelligence information for the purpose of enhancing the competitiveness or
business prospects of U.S. companies. And it has articulated its view that
established principles of international law—including those of the law of
armed conflict—do apply in cyberspace.

But beyond these very general statements, the U.S. government has
placed little on the public record, and there is little authoritative information about U.S. offensive capabilities in cyberspace, rules of engagement,
doctrine for the use of offensive capabilities, organizational responsibilities within the Department of Defense and the intelligence community,
and a host of other topics related to offensive operations.

It is likely that behind the veil of classification, these topics have been
discussed at length. But a full public discussion of issues in these areas has
yet to coalesce, and classification of such topics has left U.S. government
thinking on these issues highly opaque. Such opacity has many undesirable consequences, but one of the most important consequences is that the
role offensive capabilities could play in defending important information
technology assets of the United States cannot be discussed fully.

What is sensitive about offensive U.S. capabilities in cyberspace is
generally the fact of U.S. interest in a specific technology for cyberattack
(rather than the nature of that technology itself); fragile and sensitive
operational details that are not specific to the technologies themselves
(e.g., the existence of a covert operative in a specific foreign country, a particular vulnerability, a particular operational program); or U.S. knowledge
of the capabilities and intentions of specific adversaries. Such information
is legitimately classified but is not particularly relevant for a discussion
about what U.S. policy should be. That is, unclassified information provides a generally reasonable basis for understanding what can be done
and for policy discussions that focus primarily on what should be done.

6.2 CONCLUSION

Cybersecurity is a complex subject whose understanding requires
knowledge and expertise from multiple disciplines, including but not
limited to computer science and information technology, psychology, eco-

---

[2] Fact sheet on U.S. Cyber Command, available at http://www.stratcom.mil/
factsheets/2/Cyber_Command/, accessed March 8, 2014.

nomics, organizational behavior, political science, engineering, sociology, decision sciences, international relations, and law. In practice, although technical measures are an important element, cybersecurity is not primarily a technical matter, although it is easy for policy analysts and others to get lost in the technical details. Furthermore, what is known about cybersecurity is often compartmented along disciplinary lines, reducing the insights available from cross-fertilization.

This primer seeks to illuminate some of these connections. Most of all, it attempts to leave the reader with two central ideas. The cybersecurity problem will never be solved once and for all. Solutions to the problem, limited in scope and longevity though they may be, are at least as much nontechnical as technical in nature.

Appendixes

A

Committee Members and Staff

COMMITTEE MEMBERS

DAVID CLARK, *Chair*, is a senior research scientist at the MIT Computer Science and Artificial Intelligence Laboratory, where he has worked since receiving his Ph.D. there in 1973. Since the mid-1970s, Clark has been leading the development of the Internet; from 1981 to 1989 he acted as chief protocol architect in this development, and he chaired the Internet Activities Board. His current research looks at redefinition of the architectural underpinnings of the Internet and at the relationship of technology and architecture to economic, societal, and policy considerations. He is helping the U.S. National Science Foundation organize its Future Internet Design program. Clark is past chair of the Computer Science and Telecommunications Board of the National Research Council and has contributed to a number of studies on the societal and policy impact of computer communications. He is co-director of the MIT Communications Futures program, a project for industry collaboration and coordination along the communications value chain.

THOMAS BERSON is founder and president of Anagram Laboratories and a visiting scholar at Stanford University. He has been a researcher at IBM Research and at Xerox PARC and has been successful as a Silicon Valley entrepreneur three times. He is attracted most strongly to security issues raised at the confluence of technology, business, and world events. Berson is a student of Sun Tzu's *Art of War* and its applicability to modern information conflict. Berson was the first person to be named a fellow of the International Association for Cryptologic Research. His citation reads, "For visionary and essential service and for numerous valuable contributions to the technical, social, and commercial development of cryptology and security." Berson was an editor of the *Journal of Cryptology* for 14 years. He is a past chair of the IEEE Technical Committee on Security and Privacy and a past president of the International Association for Cryptologic Research. Berson has been a member of three previous National Research Council committees: the Committee on Computer Security in the Department of Energy, the Committee to Review DoD C4I Plans and Programs, and the Committee on Offensive Information Warfare. Berson earned a B.S. in physics from the State University of New York in 1967 and a Ph.D. in computer science from the University of London in 1977. He was a visiting fellow in mathematics in the University of Cambridge, and he is a life member of Clare Hall, Cambridge. Berson's Erdös number is 2; his amateur radio call sign is ND2T.

MARJORY BLUMENTHAL[1] became executive director of the President's Council of Advisors on Science and Technology (PCAST) in May 2013, after a decade combining academic leadership at Georgetown University with research and advisory activities (including as a RAND adjunct) aimed at understanding Internet and cybersecurity technology trends and policy implications. She stewards the council and its program of analyses (spanning science and technology) that culminate in policy recommendations to the President and the Administration. In fall 2013, PCAST published *Immediate Opportunities for Strengthening the Nation's Cybersecurity*. Blumenthal joined Georgetown University in August 2003 as associate provost, academic, engaging in campus-wide strategy and overseeing academic units and special initiatives. She led efforts to strengthen Georgetown sciences (culminating in the 2012 opening of a new science building and launch of a new computer science Ph.D. program), and she promoted innovation in teaching, launching Online@GU and co-developing the Initiative for Technology-Enhanced Learning. Between July 1987 and August 2003, Blumenthal was the director of the National Research Council's Computer Science and Telecommunications Board (CSTB). Several of the more than 60 reports produced with her leadership affected public policy and/or became trade books. Her cybersecurity work began with CSTB's influential *Computers at Risk*. Blumenthal did her undergraduate work at Brown University and received her M.S. in public policy at Harvard University.

---

[1] Ms. Blumenthal resigned from the committee on May 1, 2013.

STAFF

HERBERT S. LIN is chief scientist at the Computer Science and Telecommunications Board, National Research Council of the National Academies, where he has been the study director of major projects on public policy and information technology. These projects include a number of studies related to cybersecurity: *Cryptography's Role in Securing the Information Society* (1996); *Realizing the Potential of C4I: Fundamental Challenges* (1999); *Engaging Privacy and Information Technology in a Digital Age* (2007); *Toward a Safer and More Secure Cyberspace* (2007); *Technology, Policy, Law, and Ethics Regarding U.S. Acquisition and Use of Cyberattack Capabilities* (2009); and *Proceedings of a Workshop on Deterring Cyberattacks: Informing Strategies and Developing Options* (2010). Prior to his NRC service, he was a professional staff member and staff scientist for the House Armed Services Committee (1986-1990), where his portfolio included defense policy and arms control issues. He received his doctorate in physics from MIT.

ERIC WHITAKER is a senior program assistant at the Computer Science and Telecommunications Board of the National Research Council. Prior to joining the CSTB, he was a realtor with Long and Foster Real Estate, Inc., in the Washington, D.C., metropolitan area. Before that, he spent several years with the Public Broadcasting Service in Alexandria, Virginia, as an associate in the Corporate Support Department. He has a B.A. in communication from Hampton University.

B

Bibliography

This bibliography lists the reports from the National Research Council's Computer Science and Telecommunications Board from which this report takes much of its material. All were published by and are available from the National Academies Press, Washington, D.C.

Chapter 1

- *Computers at Risk: Safe Computing in the Information Age* (1991)
- *Toward a Safer and More Secure Cyberspace* (2007)

Chapter 2

- *Computing the Future: A Broader Agenda for Computer Science and Engineering* (1992)
- *Trust in Cyberspace* (1999)
- *Being Fluent with Information Technology* (1999)
- *The Internet's Coming of Age* (2001)
- *Signposts in Cyberspace: The Domain Name System and Internet Navigation* (2005)

Chapter 3

- *Toward a Safer and More Secure Cyberspace* (2007)
- *Technology, Policy, Law, and Ethics Regarding U.S. Acquisition and Use of Cyberattack Capabilities* (2009)

Chapter 4

- *Cryptography's Role in Securing the Information Society* (1996)
- *Who Goes There? Authentication Through the Lens of Privacy* (2003)
- *Toward a Safer and More Secure Cyberspace* (2007)
- *Technology, Policy, Law, and Ethics Regarding U.S. Acquisition and Use of Cyberattack Capabilities* (2009)
- *Toward Better Usability, Security, and Privacy of Information Technology: Report of a Workshop* (2010)
- *Letter Report from the Committee on Deterring Cyberattacks: Informing Strategies and Developing Options for U.S. Policy* (2010)

Chapter 5

- *Toward a Safer and More Secure Cyberspace* (2007)
- *Engaging Privacy and Information Technology in a Digital Age* (2007)
- *Assessing the Impacts of Changes in the Information Technology R&D Ecosystem: Retaining Leadership in an Increasingly Global Environment* (2009)
- *Technology, Policy, Law, and Ethics Regarding U.S. Acquisition and Use of Cyberattack Capabilities* (2009)

Chapter 6

- *Toward a Safer and More Secure Cyberspace* (2007)
- *Technology, Policy, Law, and Ethics Regarding U.S. Acquisition and Use of Cyberattack Capabilities* (2009)